SNOOKER

John Spencer first played snooker at the age of fourteen, and while only fifteen achieved a 115 break. His interest lapsed during National Service, however, and it was not until he was twenty-eight that he resumed playing and almost immediately joined the top amateur circuit. After turning professional, he won the World Championship title at his first attempt in 1969, regained it eighteen months later, and won it again in 1977. Since then he has won many major tournaments and has earned himself an international reputation as an elegant 'natural' player who is also one of snooker's great thinkers and tacticians.

Clive Everton, himself a professional player, is editor of *Snooker Scene* and is well known for his perceptive TV commentaries on games which have gripped the attention of millions of viewers.

TEACH YOURSELF BOOKS

SNOOKER

John Spencer

Edited by Clive Everton

TEACH YOURSELF BOOKS

Hodder and Stoughton

First published by Cassell & Co. Ltd as
Spencer on Snooker
Copyright © 1973, 1978 John Spencer
Revised and reset for the Teach Yourself series

Teach Yourself edition first published 1986
Copyright © 1986 John Spencer

Illustrations by Duncan Mil
Copyright © 1986 Hodder and Stoughton Ltd

Second impression 1986

British Library Cataloguing in Publication Data
Spencer, John
[Spencer on snooker]. Snooker
1. Snooker
I. [Spencer on snooker]   II. Title
794.7'35   GV900.S6

ISBN 0 340 39366 1

Printed and bound in Great Britain for
Hodder and Stoughton Educational,
a division of Hodder and Stoughton Ltd,
Mill Road, Dunton Green, Sevenoaks, Kent,
by Richard Clay Ltd, Bungay, Suffolk.
Photoset by Rowland Phototypesetting Ltd,
Bury St Edmunds, Suffolk

Contents

Introduction

There were three million Snooker players in the British Isles alone even before television popularised the game and transformed its image. It was, in a sense, the last of the folk sports, as its skills tended to be handed down informally rather than through structured coaching schemes.

By the mid-eighties there were seven million players in Britain and the game had transcended its traditional geographical limitations of the past and present British Commonwealth. There are now more coaches and much more thinking about coaching, and television has itself proved a fine coach. So much top class play has been shown that correct shot selection and tactics are much more quickly assimilated than they were in the pre-television age.

Teach Yourself Snooker concentrates initially on fundamental techniques – without fair mastery of which the most exhaustive knowledge of the game is virtually useless. It proceeds to a full discussion of the principles of shot selection, break-building, safety and tactical play, and in conclusion anatomises the construction of a century break.

1

Basics

The basic rules

Snooker is played with twenty-two balls, which are positioned at the start of the frame (or game) as shown in Fig. 1, with the reds forming a triangle behind the pink.

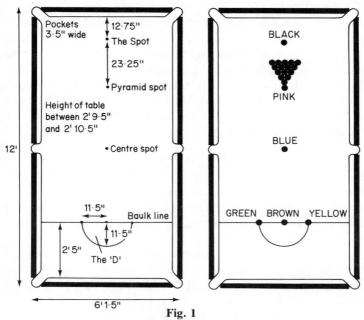

Fig. 1

The cue-ball, which is used alternately by both players, can be placed anywhere in the 'D' for the first stroke, but must thereafter be played from where it comes to rest except after an in-off or being forced off the table, in which cases the next player must again play from the 'D'.

Points are scored by the player's own potting and by his opponent conceding penalty points. Each player must first attempt to strike a red (value 1). When he pots a red he must then play at a colour, the values of which are: black (7), pink (6), blue (5), brown (4), green (3), yellow (2).

The player should nominate the colour he is attempting, although the letter of this rule is not enforced in cases where this is obvious.

If a colour is potted, it is replaced on its own spot and another red is then attempted, and so on until all fifteen reds have been potted. The colours are then taken in ascending order of value until only the cue-ball remains on the table.

If a colour cannot be replaced on its own spot (because another ball is there), it is placed on the highest-value available spot.

Failure to strike a red involves a penalty of 4 points (the minimum penalty for any foul) but the penalty is increased to 5, 6 or 7 if, instead of a red, the cue-ball strikes blue, pink or black respectively.

An in-off is a foul carrying a penalty of 4 points or more, depending on the value of the ball initially struck.

Failure to strike a nominated colour also carries a 4 point penalty, or more if the ball involved is of higher value. If, for example, green is nominated but pink is struck, the penalty is 6. If pink is nominated and green is struck, the penalty is also 6.

Snookers

Penalties often result not from incompetence or chance, but from snookers. A snooker occurs when the balls are so placed that a player cannot strike the ball he is due to play without first hitting a cushion or making the cue-ball swerve.

If a player is snookered on the reds after a foul shot by his opponent, he may nominate any coloured ball as a red. This is known as a *free ball*. If he pots it, he scores 1, the ball is re-spotted and the player can then nominate a colour in the usual way.

If no red remains, a free ball is valued at a number of points equal to that of the lowest value colour remaining and the colours are then taken in sequence. For the purpose of this rule, a player is deemed to be snookered if he cannot directly hit both extremities of the object-ball he is due to play. (The exception to this rule is when one or more reds are preventing a player striking a particular red.)

Fouls

A foul is committed:

(*a*) if a player's cue-tip strikes the cue-ball more than once in the same stroke

(*b*) if a ball is forced off the table

(*c*) if a player plays with both feet off the floor

(*d*) if a player plays before all the balls have come to rest

(*e*) if a player strikes or touches a ball other than with the tip of the cue

(*f*) by causing the cue-balls to jump over any intervening ball

(*g*) by playing with the balls wrongly spotted.

After any foul shot, whether he is entitled to a free ball or not, a player can ask his opponent to play again.

Penalties: some examples

1 The player, 'on' a red, misses it and strikes no other ball: *penalty 4* (minimum penalty).

2 The player, 'on' a red, misses it and strikes blue: *penalty 5* (the value of blue).

3 The player, 'on' pink, misses it and strikes a red: *penalty 6* (the value of pink).

4 The player, 'on' pink, misses it and strikes black: *penalty 7* (the value of black).

5 The player, 'on' a red, strikes it, but goes in-off: *penalty 4* (minimum penalty).

6 The player, 'on' blue, misses, and the cue-ball enters a pocket without contacting another ball: *penalty 5* (the value of blue).

If any ball (including the cue-ball) leaves the table, the penalty will be the *higher* value of (*a*) the ball 'on' or (*b*) the ball actually leaving the table, if different. The minimum penalty is 4. If the cue-ball leaves the table, it is replaced in the 'D'. Colours are re-spotted, but reds remain off the table.

If, when playing a red, two or more reds are potted, *no foul is committed* and 1 point is scored for each red pocketed. Potting a red and a colour, or two colours, from a single stroke constitutes a foul, however, and any colours so potted are replaced on their spots.

The general rule is that the penalty awarded is the highest numerical value of the ball 'on' or fouled, with a minimum penalty of 4 and a maximum penalty of 7 points. Penalty points are not subtracted from the offender's score but are credited to his opponent.

Some common terms

Break: A sequence of scoring shots.

Break-off: The first shot of a frame in which the striker plays at the unbroken triangle of reds.

Clear the table: A sequence of shots in which a player pots all the balls left on the table.

Double: A shot by which a ball enters a pocket after striking one or more cushions (see p. 110).

Maximum break: A sequence of shots in which a player takes all fifteen reds, fifteen blacks and all the colours to score 147.

Plant: A position in which the first object-ball is played on to the second object-ball in such a way as to make the second ball enter the pocket (see p. 115).

Safety shot: A shot in which a player makes no attempt to score but intends to leave his opponent unable to score (see Chapter 4).

Screw: Reverse spin or backspin. This is applied by striking the cue-ball well below centre (see p. 23).

Set: A position in which two object-balls are touching in such a way that the second ball is certain to be potted however the first object-ball is struck (see p. 115).

Shot to nothing: A position in which a player attempts a pot in such a way as to leave himself in position to continue his break if successful, but will leave the cue-ball in a safe position for his opponent if unsuccessful (see p. 79).

Side: Sidespin. This is applied by striking the cue-ball to either the right or left of centre (see p. 28).

Stun: A shot in which the cue-ball is stopped dead (if the pot is straight) by striking the cue-ball just below centre. If the pot is not straight, the stun shot is used to widen the angle the cue-ball takes after potting the object-ball (see p. 26).

It is impossible to play snooker well if you are not in the right frame of mind. After a certain standard, it is not technique which makes one player better than another, but his psychological approach to the game. Confidence is the most important asset a player can have.

The cue

Confidence starts as early as choosing a cue. Because no two pieces of timber are exactly the same, no two cues are exactly the same. Therefore, all professionals and good amateurs play with one cue all the time.

How do you choose a cue? If a stranger walks into a billiards room, the chances are that you will see him take a cue out of the rack and roll it across the table to see if it is straight and 'true'. The cue with which I won my first two World Championships would never have passed this test. It was nowhere near straight, but I had always played with it and felt lost playing with any other. The butt was jagged and battered as if a couple of dogs had been gnawing at it, and it was held together by a nail. It weighed only 15 ozs – most experts say that 17 ozs is the best weight for a snooker cue – and many people had told me that I would be a better player with a heavier cue. I doubted this because my cue felt so right that it gave me confidence. Therefore my advice in choosing a cue is to trust your own instinct and common sense.

Nevertheless, if you buy a cue of your own buy a straight one, because this in itself is a pyschological boost. Unless you've played with the same cue for years, you might think when playing with a bent cue that you are hitting the ball straight but the pots aren't going in because the cue is warped or twisted. You blame the cue instead of yourself.

As it happened, I was forced into a change of cue because my old trusty was broken in a car accident. The three pieces were pinned together by a miraculous bit of cue surgery and I even won a couple of events with the re-built cue, but it never really felt right. I tried a couple of other cues but couldn't settle down with them, and it was not until I tried a Canadian two-piece that I again felt that I had a cue I could play well with. In fact, I won the 1977 World Championship with it. Subsequently, I switched to a Japanese two-piece which, like the Canadian one, is 17 ozs. I think if I was starting from scratch I would use a two-piece, because they are so much easier to carry about. It is also possible to buy two shafts with every butt. This in effect gives you a spare cue if you have tip trouble with one shaft.

I would say you couldn't improve on a cue which feels right, is about 4 ft 10 in. long, and tapers down to 10 or 11 mm at the tip, but don't take my word as final. Of course you *can* improve your play by changing your cue, but in most cases if it feels right, it is right.

Many beginners go wrong as soon as they pick up a cue by gripping it at the very end. Cues are balanced in such a way that they should be gripped about 2 or 3 inches from the end. Again, the grip which makes you feel most comfortable is probably the best grip for you. Don't be afraid to experiment but, if you pick up the cue as if you were going to clout somebody over the head, the chances are you will grip it in about the right position for snooker.

Stance

Assuming you are a right-handed player playing straight up or across the table, as if potting a straight blue in the middle pocket, stand at approximately 45° to the table, right foot pointing, as you stand, at an angle of about 45°. The left leg should be slightly bent and the right leg should be straight. Your feet should be about a foot apart. The main thing is to be comfortable and have a firm, solid stance (without being too rigid) so that your body does not move when you are hitting the ball (Fig. 2). The only part of the body which should move as you hit the ball is the lower right arm, that is from elbow to wrist. In practice I don't think I stand the same for every shot, but I've never worried about it.

Still standing sideways, you lower your left hand onto the table to form a *bridge* about nine inches from the cue-ball. Cock your thumb to form a tight channel with your first finger so that the cue rests on your thumb and first finger and not between them. A beginner's bridge is invariably wobbly and insecure, but gradually the muscles of the hand will develop enough to enable him to form a firm bridge without even thinking.

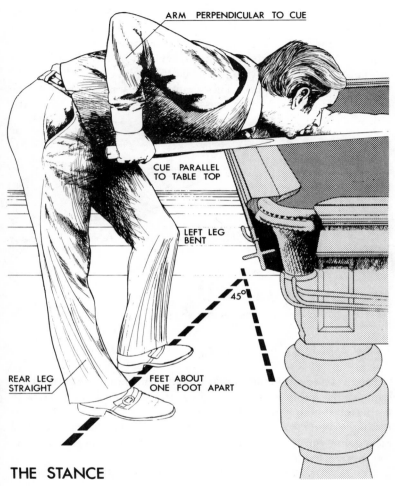

ARM PERPENDICULAR TO CUE

CUE PARALLEL
TO TABLE TOP

LEFT LEG
BENT

45°

REAR LEG
STRAIGHT

FEET ABOUT
ONE FOOT APART

THE STANCE

Fig. 2

There are hundreds of small variations in the way a bridge can be made. It has always been said that the fingers of the bridge hand should be spread as widely as possible, the theory being, I suppose, that the wider the base, the firmer the bridge. I would agree with this except to emphasise that this spread should be only as wide as is comfortably possible.

In my own case, my first finger is almost tucked under my thumb (see Fig. 3) so that my cue is running across it. I don't say that this is the correct way, but it seems to suit me. It doesn't suit me to wear a watch or ring on my left hand; it just feels wrong. My other fingers are flat with the ends gripping the cloth firmly. Some players play with their fingers bunched. This seems to suit some people, but the danger of bunching the fingers is that you sometimes can't sight the ball so clearly.

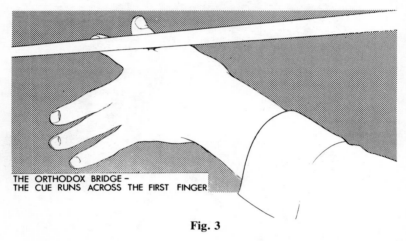

THE ORTHODOX BRIDGE –
THE CUE RUNS ACROSS THE FIRST FINGER

Fig. 3

Joe Davis recommended that the left arm should be pushed out straight, but if this feels unnatural – as it does to me – then play with the left arm bent. From elbow to hand, the whole of my left arm is resting on the table as I play a shot. Once again, this is how I feel most comfortable. Being comfortable is the basis of all good play on the snooker table.

As you settle down to play your shot, your cue should be brushing the middle of the point of your chin. Joe Davis used to run his cue underneath his left eye; as his right eye was very weak, this made him a special case.

Cue action

In preparing to address the cue-ball, the cue should be running as level as possible and sighting along the line of the shot. If the butt of

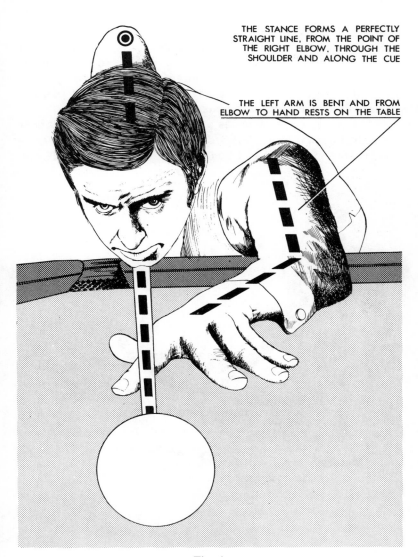

THE STANCE FORMS A PERFECTLY
STRAIGHT LINE, FROM THE POINT OF
THE RIGHT ELBOW, THROUGH THE
SHOULDER AND ALONG THE CUE

THE LEFT ARM IS BENT AND FROM
ELBOW TO HAND RESTS ON THE TABLE

Fig. 4

the cue is raised, any spin imparted to the ball, intentionally or unintentionally, is exaggerated, as the cue-ball is struck with a downwards motion.

Some of my technically-minded friends in snooker have told me that I have a perfect alignment in that cue, upper arm and elbow are in a straight line, with the lower arm, from elbow to wrist, perpendicular (see Fig. 4). But unlike many experts I believe that, of these, a perfect elbow to wrist is the most important.

If you think of the elbow as a hinge, the lower arm will move naturally backwards and forwards a few degrees from the perpendicular (Fig. 5). But if you hold the cue too near the end, your

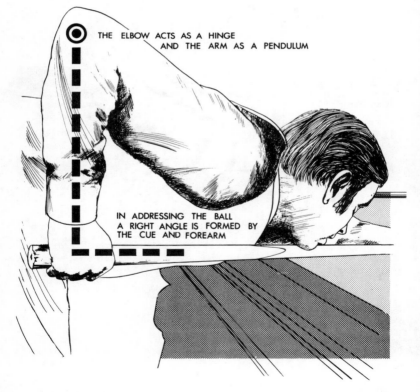

THE ELBOW ACTS AS A HINGE
AND THE ARM AS A PENDULUM

IN ADDRESSING THE BALL
A RIGHT ANGLE IS FORMED BY
THE CUE AND FOREARM

Fig. 5

forward movement will only jerk your lower arm just about as far as the perpendicular and will be bound to make your cue action a see-saw, up and down affair which can't possibly be any good to you.

I believe that anybody can develop this perpendicular lower arm without much trouble, but the alignment of cue, upper arm and elbow is something which, unless you drop into as naturally as I did, is very difficult to acquire.

Logically, from a mechanical point of view, you are more likely to hit straight if the force of the blow is applied directly from behind. On the other hand, there are many players who have a 'parallel' action. If any expert tells you that it is impossible to play good snooker with your elbow sticking out and the wrist turned outwards, you should remind him that this action was good enough for Ray Reardon to win the World Championship six times.

In short, as long as your cueing is in the groove I don't believe it really matters which groove it is. Even if it does matter, I think that this alignment is so difficult to achieve that it is not worth the effort. Under pressure, it is the manufactured rather than the natural skills which let players down.

Complete beginners can practise their cue action by placing the cue-ball on the brown spot and aiming over the blue, pink and black spots to bring the ball back on the same line after hitting the top cushion. Do this slowly at first and then work up to medium pace, enough for the cue-ball to travel three lengths of the table.

If you can get the cue-ball to keep to this line, allowing an inch or so either way, you can be satisfied that you are cueing well enough to try something a little more ambitious.

Don't try to hit the ball hard to start with, but concentrate on developing a nice easy action. You should be addressing the ball with a few preliminary approaches like a golfer lining up a putt. At the end of the last preliminary backswing there should be a very brief but definite pause before the cue is actually thrust forward at the ball.

A lot of players 'feather' at the cue-ball almost imperceptibly before exploding into action with a sudden attack at the ball. They should be using these preliminary addresses to build up rhythm and straight cueing.

While you are doing this, your eyes are switching between three points: the spot of the cue-ball which you want your tip to hit, the spot of the object-ball you want the cue-ball to hit, and the pocket, which is, of course, where you want the object-ball to go.

I am not certain just where my eyes are looking at a particular stage of my address and I don't think it really matters. After they have sighted the angle some people feather two or three times at the cue-ball without looking at the object-ball, just to reassure themselves that they are cueing correctly. Other players switch their eyes like a yo-yo from cue-ball to object-ball to coincide with the backward and forward motion of their cue.

The only definite piece of advice I would offer is that in the instant before you strike the cue-ball you should be looking steadily at the object-ball.

There is no set number of preliminary addresses you should make. I make between four and six, as do most players, though some, like Alex Higgins, make theirs more quickly.

Each player, in fact, will develop his own tempo. The trick is to use the time you are addressing the cue-ball to set yourself for the shot until you are perfectly still. A man firing a rifle doesn't fling himself on the ground and fire as soon as he sees the target. He settles himself until he has the bullseye steadily in his sights and then fires.

Instinctive first-time sighting is a great asset but of very little value if the player moves in making his shot. I think a player is less likely to move on his shot if he has settled himself for a couple of seconds than if he is bobbing up and down like a yo-yo. Higgins, of course, has proved an exception to this rule, thus emphasising again that natural ability outweighs what appear to be technical faults.

At the other extreme, players who play very slowly can handicap themselves through expending too much concentration on each shot. As soon as you have found what you think is the correct angle to hit the ball and are perfectly still, play the shot. Like the rifleman, you will find that the longer you try to hold a still position the more likely you are to miss.

It is natural to give vital shots extra care, but excessive care (which shows itself in making more preliminary addresses than usual) is generally just as fatal as not enough care.

Basic technique

Many pundits favour a short backswing on the theory that the shorter distance the cue moves, the less likely it is to deviate from a straight course. There is something in this argument.

On the other hand, the shorter your backswing the more limited you are in your range of shots. In cricket, a batsman with a short backswing is more likely to hit the ball than someone with a long backswing, but he is unlikely to hit it as far.

With a short backswing it is virtually impossible to play long run-throughs and deep screws to championship standard. In trying to generate the necessary power, a player with a short backswing will invariably tend to snatch or jerk so that the tip of his cue finishes up pointing at the roof.

There have been players whose natural ability has carried them through this kind of limitation to some extent. They either have to make a big effort to change their game or make do with what they have.

As a general guide, only go out of your way to change a part of your game if it seems unlikely that you will ever get much better without doing so.

Improving your game

Most snooker instructional books have been written with the theory that readers are prepared to spend hundreds of hours practising by themselves.

You do find some dedicated characters for whom nothing is too much trouble, but most of Britain's seven million players want to play a little better without having to put in more effort than they feel inclined, or have time for. In fact, the surest way to throw away any natural ability you might have been born with is to make snooker hard work.

There are plenty of good players about who were born with little natural ability, so it is possible to improve a great deal with systematic practice and concentration. But as soon as a player becomes obsessed with technique, he has written his own death warrant.

Therefore, if you can master the basic skills of snooker in your own way, be satisfied with that. Don't go chasing after the illusion of perfect technique. You should be directing all your mental energy outwards – towards winning – rather than inwards, when you will often beat yourself through setting your performance against some arbitrary standards of perfection. By all means look at good players and incorporate small points naturally into your game, but never strain to make your style a carbon copy of someone else's.

For instance, you might experiment with varying the length of your bridge for certain shots. When I play a close shot (with the cue-ball and object-ball less than 3 ft apart) my bridge is much closer to the cue-ball than if the object-ball were more distant (see Fig. 6). I find a long bridge to a short shot is uncomfortable but that a long bridge to a long shot enables me to see the angle more clearly and sight the pot better.

Try to relax when you are playing. The ideal is to be perfectly relaxed physically but very alert mentally. There are hundreds of players who seem to be able to pot anything in a friendly knockabout but produce only a shadow of their form in a match. This is because nervous tension causes certain muscles to stiffen, particularly in the arm. Instead of the lower arm swinging freely from the elbow, tension often sets in to such a degree that a player starts getting his shoulder into the shot, 'throwing' the elbow outwards and causing the shot to be missed.

The ability to stay relaxed in a match is usually natural rather than manufactured, but experience can improve a player's temperament considerably. Play as many matches as you can. Friendly games are fine for general improvement in potting and positional play but the important thing, in the long run, is how well you can play when it really matters whether you win or lose.

Some people play above their normal form in front of a big crowd, some play below. Concentration is the key to it all. When I feel my own concentration starting to wander, I make sure that, when my opponent is at the table, my eyes never leave the cue-ball.

When it's your turn to play, remember one thing above everything else. Keep still. If your body is moving sideways on a shot, it is impossible to get it unless you have aimed wrongly in the first place. If your body is moving forward, you are inevitably changing your sighting of both cue-ball and object-ball in mid-shot. Using the comparison with a rifle again, you might possibly hit your target while the gun is moving, but you have a much better chance of doing so if it is still.

Keeping still on the shot is the most important part of playing well. You can do a lot of things wrong which often won't matter if only you keep still. Keep your head down. If you do, you will usually find that the rest of your body will stay still of its own accord.

You must have confidence in the way that you play the game, as well. A lot of so-called experts try to analyse the naturalness out of

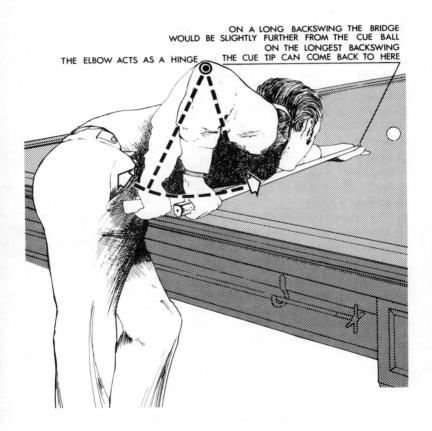

ON A LONG BACKSWING THE BRIDGE
WOULD BE SLIGHTLY FURTHER FROM THE CUE BALL
ON THE LONGEST BACKSWING
THE ELBOW ACTS AS A HINGE   THE CUE TIP CAN COME BACK TO HERE

Fig. 6

any sport, but if you can do something well, why worry about how you do it? Study it by all means, but in my experience, players who are obsessed with technique never reach the very top. Of course you must have an appreciation of broad principles, but too much analysis usually leads to a player analysing all his natural ability out of himself and leaving a manufactured article which isn't as good as the original.

My own game is completely natural: although I know that I don't always stand in exactly the same position, I hit the ball now exactly as I always have. My improvement has come in shot selection, in a greater range of shots, in recognising situations which have cropped up before, and in confidence in my game. Although I practised a lot when I first started, I tried never to make hard work of it by practising one shot for hours at a time. It is unnatural to play one shot out of context of the game as a whole. This only gives a particular shot an unnatural emphasis and puts more pressure on you when it occurs.

Potting

I've read all sorts of theories about potting – or at least I've started to read them until they became too complicated. Remember that snooker is a ball game and that most people are born with a greater or lesser degree of ball sense.

To pot a ball at snooker, you have a cue-ball, an object-ball and a pocket. If the three are in a straight line then you must succeed if the cue-ball hits the object-ball full in the face. If they are not in a straight line then obviously you have to hit the object-ball at a certain angle in order to pot it. The main thing to remember here is that you want the cue-ball to make contact with the object-ball at the point diametrically opposite the pocket. Many beginners forget to make allowance for the half-diameter of the cue-ball which represents the difference between the points of aim and contact.

If you haven't got a basic judgment of angles, you will never pot very well. Most people with normal eyesight do have this judgment and, as they play more and more, will recognise, through trial and error, the correct angle to hit the ball.

In fact, the most important part of potting is memory. One

half-ball pot is the same as another, regardless of where the balls may be situated. Although there are an infinite number of different positions, the number of potting angles is limited.

You should be selecting the angle at which you are going to hit the object-ball as you are walking to the table. It is not a bad idea to walk to the table as far as possible *on the line of the shot*.

Therefore, once you have got down to take your shot you should need to adjust your aim only slightly. The worst thing you can do is to get down before you have thought what you are going to do. Players who do this can be seen radically altering their aim without changing the position of their feet or re-aligning their body. This sort of alteration inevitably leads to a player hitting across the cue-ball and considerably reduces his chances of getting the pot. If you do alter your mind after you have got down, get up and start your preparation of the shot again.

But to go back to my point about potting being largely memory, you can't use your memory unless there is something to remember. In short, you must, through trial and error, get the feel of potting balls from different angles so that, in time, your eyes will recognise the angle when it crops up again.

One exercise I can recommend for beginners is simply to pot the black off its spot from as many different angles as possible.

Potting the black from its spot is so important in break-building that any ambitious player must regard this as a shot which he must never miss, from any angle. Therefore, starting with a straight pot, place the cue-ball at different points in turn until you have covered the complete range of angles. Do this from both sides of the table so that you don't develop too much of a preference for one side.

Not quite so basic

If you have already reached a certain standard you will have realised that the simple basic rules with which one begins have to be varied in certain circumstances.

It is impossible, for instance, always to bridge in the orthodox manner.

Figure 7 shows how I bridge when the cue-ball is too near the cushion for me to comfortably get my hand on the table and swing

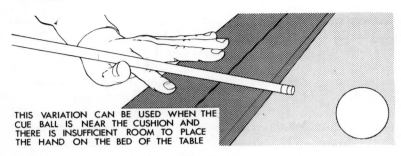

THIS VARIATION CAN BE USED WHEN THE
CUE BALL IS NEAR THE CUSHION AND
THERE IS INSUFFICIENT ROOM TO PLACE
THE HAND ON THE BED OF THE TABLE

Fig. 7

naturally. I tuck the thumb away and spread my first finger over to
the right and leave a channel for the cue between the first and
second fingers. My fingertips come right up to the edge of the
cushion.

In a similar position or, more often, when the cue-ball is nearer
the cushion, I sometimes use a bridge with the heel of the hand
slightly below the level of the cushion rail and the cue running
between the V formed by the thumb and first finger and along the
cushion rail.

When the cue-ball is much closer to the cushion (see Fig. 8), I
take my bridge hand back further still, especially if the object-ball is
more than a couple of feet away, so that only my fingers are
supporting my arm.

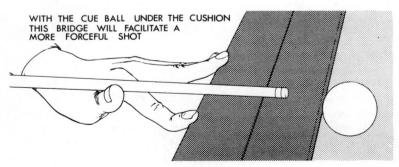

WITH THE CUE BALL UNDER THE CUSHION
THIS BRIDGE WILL FACILITATE A
MORE FORCEFUL SHOT

Fig. 8

If the object-ball is very close to the cushion and if I need only to hit the ball softly, I make a shorter but firmer bridge, but I cannot hit the ball with much strength unless I give myself a reasonable distance between the bridge and the object-ball.

This principle shows itself in Fig. 9 where, again, I play with the tips of my fingers very close to the cue-ball unless the object-ball is some distance away, when I need to lengthen my bridge to enable me to get the cue-ball and object-ball in the same line of vision.

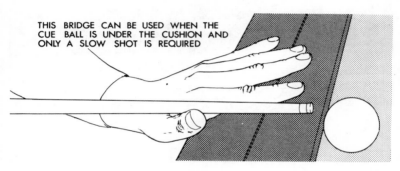

THIS BRIDGE CAN BE USED WHEN THE CUE BALL IS UNDER THE CUSHION AND ONLY A SLOW SHOT IS REQUIRED

Fig. 9

One of the most effective safety shots is to leave one's opponent right under the cushion. He has only the top part of the cue-ball to aim at; it is impossible to use screw or stun and very difficult indeed even for a professional to use side with any control.

The first objective when playing from under a cushion is to avoid a miscue. As there is such a small part of the cue-ball to hit, the very edge of the tip just misses or just catches as the main part of the tip hits the cue-ball.

A player has only got to lift his head, or cue not quite perfectly, and his tip will either skim across the top of the cue-ball or hit the cushion before the ball – producing a miscue either way.

Other bridges which one sometimes needs to use include the one shown in Fig. 10. I hold my first finger over my thumb to form a loop. The cue goes through this loop and is kept in a straight line by the second finger.

The second and third fingers are supporting the hand on the table while the little finger, because there isn't room to get it comfortably on the table, is tucked out of the way on the cushion.

Bridging over an intervening ball is an important ability to master because, with so many balls scattered about a snooker table, it is inevitable that this position will arise often.

THE 'LOOP' BRIDGE CAN BE USED WHEN THE
CUSHION PREVENTS AN ORTHODOX BRIDGE

Fig. 10

As Fig. 11 shows, the cue must be raised to avoid fouling the intervening ball. The nearer the cue-ball is to the intervening ball, the harder it is to strike the cue-ball well. If the cue-ball is tight against the intervening ball, the bridge hand has to be brought nearer and the angle made even steeper to strike the relatively small part of the cue-ball which is still visible.

In the drawing, there are a couple of inches between the intervening ball and the cue-ball but the angle of the cue is still pretty steep.

The bridge is supported by all four fingers and occasionally I get extra support by resting the point of my elbow on the cushion.

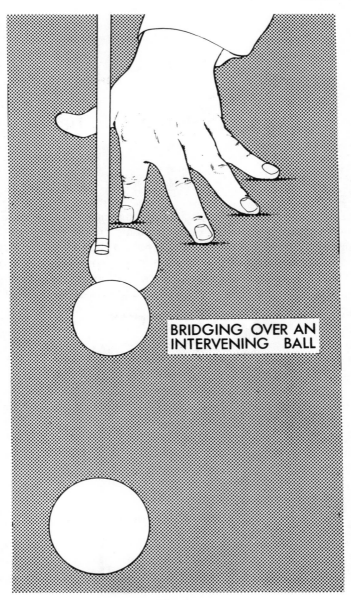

BRIDGING OVER AN
INTERVENING BALL

Fig. 11

2

Controlling the Cue-ball

After you have passed the beginner's stage at which you need all your concentration to get even the quite simple pots, you can progress to positional play – playing pots in such a way as to leave yourself in the best possible position to play your following shot.

The first positional technique – often overlooked – is gauging the strength or weight of shot. In Fig. 1, the idea is to pot the black to

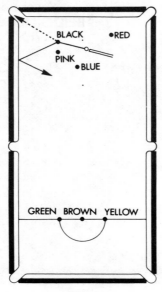

Fig. 1

gain position on the last red. Play the shot too slow and the cue-ball will finish on the side cushion, snookered by the pink; play it too hard and it will finish behind the blue.

No matter how good your control of strength, however, you cannot achieve much of a standard without being able to use screw, stun and side and – often overlooked again – top.

Topspin

By striking the cue-ball *above* centre you are imparting topspin. This accentuates the ball's natural forward motion and causes it to run further than it would if struck lower. When using top, raise your bridge slightly so that you can strike the top of the cue-ball with a natural swing, with the cue parallel to the bed of the table.

Backspin (screw)

By striking the cue-ball *below* centre you are *counteracting* the ball's natural forward motion by imparting backspin. If the cue-ball is struck below centre, it skids towards the object-ball, rotating backwards. When it contacts the object-ball, its natural forward movement is halted and the backspin will cause the cue-ball to spring back.

How is this backspin, or screw, applied?

To get the best results, tilt or lower your bridge hand slightly, so that your cue tip can strike lower at the cue-ball without having to point downwards. If you fail to do this, your eyes tend to be looking into the bed of the table instead of along the line of the shot. Your follow-through, which is very important, will also be restricted if your cue is sloping down, since it must come in contact with the cloth if it hits straight through the ball. If it doesn't, it means that you cannot be following through properly and that you are some-how jerking or pulling at your shot. Tilting or lowering your bridge will enable you to keep your cue parallel to the table.

Having done this, place a ball on the blue spot and the cue-ball a foot from it (as shown in Fig. 2). Point the cue-tip about halfway between the centre of the ball and the bed of the table, and build up

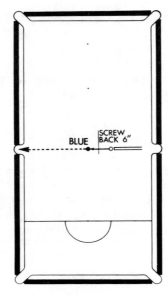

Fig. 2

a rhythm by making a few preliminary addresses at the ball. Then, pot the object-ball and try to screw back six inches.

To do so, you need only strike the object-ball hard enough to travel two widths of the table. You should not need to strike it hard enough to travel three widths.

A lot of players never master the screw shot simply because they get tense at the thought of it. They are so conscious that a screw shot is 'different' from a plain ball shot that, instead of addressing the ball in a relaxed natural way, they take one sudden nervous jab at it and hope for the best.

The most common fault of all is hitting too hard. A lot of players find difficulty in screwing back and try to compensate by hitting harder. In fact, their failure to screw back can usually be traced to failing to strike the cue-ball where they think they are striking it, or failing to follow-through properly.

By playing this short, six-inch screwback several times, a player will gradually acquire the 'feel' of a screw shot and develop the

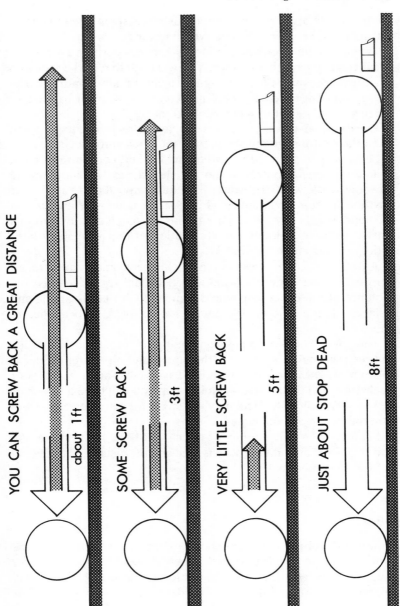

YOU CAN SCREW BACK A GREAT DISTANCE

about 1ft

SOME SCREW BACK

3ft

VERY LITTLE SCREW BACK

5ft

JUST ABOUT STOP DEAD

8ft

Fig. 3

confidence to attempt more ambitious screw shots. Don't start by hitting hard, because if you do, you'll never get the rhythm.

When you can screw back six inches from this position every time, see if you can screw back a foot. You will need to play the shot with slightly more power but, again, guard against really clouting it. The important thing to remember is that it is no use screwing back a foot when you only want to screw back six inches.

Once you can do this, you will soon find yourself able to pot a ball from the centre spot and screw back into the centre pocket.

As you try to screw back further and further, concentrate all the time on playing a controlled shot. Some players, when attempting to screw back what they think is a long way, tend to lose their rhythm in their preliminary addresses, as if they believe that a tremendously hard hit is required. This approach usually ends in a final convulsive jerk and the elimination of that vital slight hesitation I wrote about on page 11.

A proficient golfer doesn't take his club back quickly and bring it forward in one continuous motion. If he did try to do this, the violence of the backswing would completely upset his timing and balance. The classic golfing advice 'slowly back' also applies to snooker.

The power of a shot comes from timing and the speed with which the cue is brought forward. On the other hand, the faster the cue is taken back, the more abruptly it will have to stop at the end of your backswing and the more certain it is that you will have a snatch or jerk in your action. Immediately you strain for extra power you will lose the key to all ball games – timing.

Figure 3 shows the interacting effects of where the tip strikes the cue-ball, what amount of speed is used and the distance the cue-ball is from the object-ball.

Stun

Whereas the object of a screw shot is to bring the cue-ball back, the object of a stun shot is to stop the cue-ball dead.

If you have absorbed the basic information in Fig. 3, you will appreciate that stopping the cue-ball dead required you to hit so low and hard that the cue-ball would screw back a considerable distance if the object-ball was nearer. Thus, you will need to strike the cue-ball higher or lower in accordance with the distance between the cue-ball and the object-ball.

In Fig. 4, for example, cue-ball and object-ball are only three inches apart. You will need to strike above centre and give the cue-ball only a sharp tap (with very little back-swing or follow-through) to stop the ball dead.

As the distance between cue-ball and object-ball increases, it will become necessary for the tip to strike lower and lower. This adjustment is again a matter of memory and experience.

Another function of stun – which is more important because it affects more shots – is that it can be used to modify the angle at which the cue-ball leaves an object-ball on any shot which is not straight.

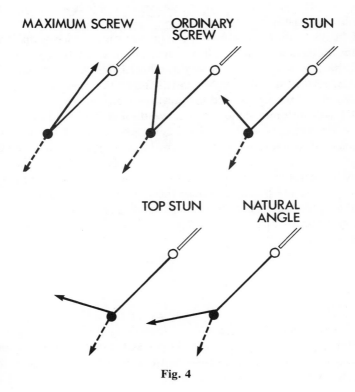

Fig. 4

Figure 5, a three-quarter-ball black off its spot, shows in line A the path the cue-ball will follow if played at a natural plain ball angle. Line E shows the line the cue-ball will follow if the shot is played with maximum screw. The lines in between show a range of possibilities varying between line D (more than a stun but not quite a full-blooded screw), through line C (a stun striking exactly halfway up the ball), to line B (a 'top stun' which takes the cue-ball off only slightly wider than its natural angle).

Being able to control the exact degree of stun and screw required is simply a matter of touch and practice. One way to acquire this is to place a red at the end of each line A, B, C, D and E and then play to pot the black and cannon gently onto each red in turn. In completing each cannon, try not to send the second object-ball more than a couple of inches. In a game situation you would, after all, be playing for the cue-ball to finish where the second object-ball is and not three feet past it.

The illustration shows how the degree of stun and screw may vary from the ordinary plain ball pot. Maximum screw brings the cue-ball back at a very narrow angle, whereas less screw widens the angle. As the tip strikes higher and higher on the cue-ball, so its final position will be further and further forward.

As will become obvious when we discuss advanced positional play, this is the type of position I generally like to be in round the black spot, because it leaves so many possibilities open for the next shot.

A lot of rubbish can be talked about 'pinpoint positional play'. There are some positions where there is only one positional shot 'on' and that one only with a very small margin of error. But in general the art of positional play is to leave oneself a *number* of possibilities.

Sidespin

Sidespin (or side) is applied by the tip striking the cue-ball either to the left or right of centre. It is used to make the cue-ball take a wider or narrower angle from a cushion than would be the case if the cue-ball was struck in the centre.

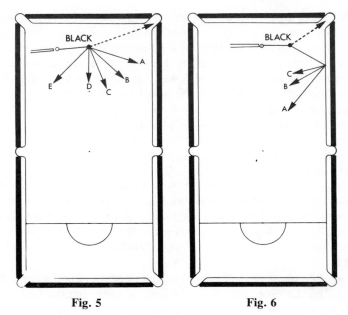

Fig. 5   **Fig. 6**

Figure 6 shows a simple pot played, in turn, with right-hand (running) side (A), plain ball (B), and with left-hand (check) side (C). The running side (A) widens the angle and the check side (C) narrows the angle at which the cue-ball leaves the cushion.

With a plain ball shot, the cue-ball will leave the cushion at the same angle at which it struck it, although the 'slide' on newly recovered cushions does widen this natural angle until they have been thoroughly 'played in'.

Potting with side is more difficult for three reasons:

(*a*) The eyes become adjusted to sighting pots through the centre of the cue-ball, whether low, middle or high.

(*b*) If left-hand side is used, the cue-ball pushes itself fractionally out to the right before spinning to the left. If right-hand side is used, the cue-ball pushes itself fractionally out to the left before spinning to the right.

(*c*) Side acts slightly differently according to the type of cloth on the table and the direction of the shot.

All these difficulties are increased in the case of those players – and there are thousands of them – who use side unintentionally when believing they are striking a plain ball shot.

The biggest fault with using side is that players forget to follow-through. This stabbing action tends to produce a swerve effect.

In time, you will overcome the difficulties of (*a*) through playing and practice – provided you are cueing correctly.

One very common fault is for players to settle down for a shot, address the cue-ball in the middle, and only then realise that they need to use side. Then, without altering their bridge, they point their cue tip to one side of the ball.

This invariably leads to the shot being missed, because the cue is hitting the cue-ball obliquely, thus making it swerve as it travels towards the object-ball. To compensate for this, some players try to hit straight by bringing the cue closer to their bodies, thus throwing their elbow and shoulder out and disturbing their natural alignment.

The difficulties of (*b*) can also be minimised by cueing correctly, that is, by the tip of the cue hitting straight through the ball.

Using medium pace, side should not have any effect on a pot if your cueing is all it should be. Be particularly careful about keeping your cue parallel to the table, as hitting downwards with side will produce a swerve.

A slow shot with side can be treacherous and is not to be recommended, except as a last resort, if the object-ball is a considerable distance from the cue-ball. As I have said, side takes the cue-ball off its natural course, so the greater the distance between the cue-ball and object-ball the more judgment is required.

The difficulties of (*c*) arise through a snooker cloth having a nap which runs from the baulk end towards the black spot. Run your hand on the table a few inches *towards* the black spot (with the nap) and the cloth will feel smooth; run it for a few inches *away from* the black spot; that is, against the nap, and it will feel rough.

All I have said about side so far refers to playing *with* the nap. Playing *against* the nap, a cue-ball carrying left-hand side will push out initially to the right and *continue* pushing to the right (see comparative illustrations in Fig. 7).

Slow shots with side against the nap should be avoided like the plague.

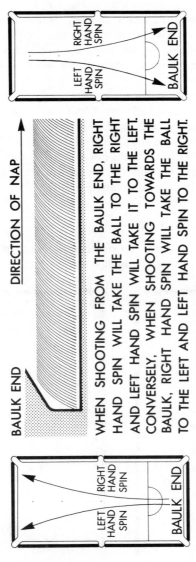

DIRECTION OF NAP

BAULK END

WHEN SHOOTING FROM THE BAULK END, RIGHT HAND SPIN WILL TAKE THE BALL TO THE RIGHT AND LEFT HAND SPIN WILL TAKE IT TO THE LEFT. CONVERSELY, WHEN SHOOTING TOWARDS THE BAULK, RIGHT HAND SPIN WILL TAKE THE BALL TO THE LEFT AND LEFT HAND SPIN TO THE RIGHT.

RIGHT HAND SPIN

LEFT HAND SPIN

BAULK END

RIGHT HAND SPIN

LEFT HAND SPIN

BAULK END

THE EFFECT OF THE NAP

Fig. 7

When cue-ball and object-ball are more than two feet apart, slow shots with side *across* the nap can all too easily go wrong. Cloths are of many different qualities and have many stages of wear, each of which produces minute variations in the effect of side.

I don't want to make the game seem harder than it is because, as a player gains experience, he adjusts to the individual characteristics of each table he plays on.

The one golden rule in all situations, though, is the greater the distance between cue-ball and object-ball, the more carefully you should think about using side.

Does the use of side have any effect on the object-ball? This is the question I am asked several times a week. My opinion is that you can impart side to an *object-ball* only unintentionally and not in a way that you can gain any advantage from it.

Combining screw and side

For advanced players, screw and side can be used simultaneously.

For instance, in Fig. 8, an ordinary screw shot will rebound off the

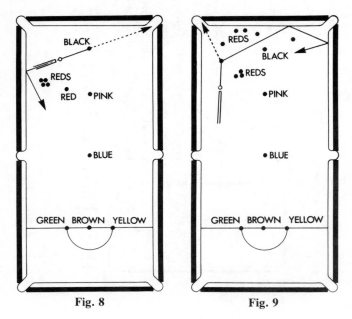

Fig. 8   Fig. 9

cushion and kiss the reds – effectively ending the break. By screwing back with screw and *left*-hand side, however, the cue-ball will rebound off the cushion at a wider angle, leaving position on the red. In this way, when screwing back, side appears to act in reverse, right-hand side swinging the cue-ball to the left as it hits the cushion and left-hand side to the right. The reason for this is that when screwing back with left-hand side you are causing the ball to spin clockwise, which is exactly the same as playing from the other side of the black spot with left-hand side.

Figure 9 shows another useful combination of screw and side where it is easy to pot the red but not so easy to obtain position on the black because of the other reds near the top cushion. Play to avoid these by potting the red with screw and right-hand side, screwing just enough for the cue-ball to miss the red nearest the black spot. This is quite a delicate shot as a little right-hand (running) side is also needed to avoid the kiss with the red near the opposite corner pocket. This running side adds speed to the cue-ball after it strikes the cushion, so the pot should be played quite softly but at the same time just sharply enough to be sure that the screw will still operate.

3

Positional Play

Beyond a very elementary standard, positional play is what the game is all about. Basically, it is the art of potting a ball in such a way as to leave the cue-ball well placed to continue the break. There are refinements of this simple principle which involve thinking several shots ahead instead of just one or two, but, to start, let's look at a stage of the game which is often crucial.

Clearing the colours

All the reds have been potted and only the colours, with a combined value of 27 points, remain. This is only six balls, and the fifteen reds and perhaps eight or ten colours have been potted. Despite this, I would say that well over half of all league games are not decided until the colours stage. If you're 26 behind it's quite possible to win if you keep your head, and if you're 26 in front it's all too easy to lose if you don't.

Let's assume your opponent has gone in-off, that all the colours are on their spots and you need all the balls to win.

Many players go wrong in this position even before they have hit the ball when, in order to make absolutely sure of potting the yellow, they place the cue-ball to leave a straight pot into the centre pocket. They then roll the yellow into the pocket so that the cue-ball runs through a few inches – to leave a possible pot green admittedly, but a rather awkward thin cut from which it is difficult to hold position for the brown.

The idea of making the yellow slightly more difficult than it need be is to make it easy for you to retain position right up to the black. By leaving yourself a slightly harder green, you are risking the possibility not only of missing the green but of not being able to get position on the brown. What often happens is that a player gradually loses position with successive shots until he leaves himself so far out of position that he misses. But by playing the first shot, the yellow, correctly you make it relatively simple to clear the table without much trouble.

Already, almost without noticing it, you are in the midst of planning more than one shot ahead; not just how to pot the yellow and stay on the green, but in such a way as to make it easy to pot the green and get on the brown.

As shown in Fig. 1, you should place the cue-ball slightly off straight, almost three-quarter ball in fact, so that the cue-ball stays in the middle of the table.

Pots of this kind tend most often to be missed by the object-ball striking the near jaw. Average players tend to exaggerate the angle of nearly straight pots, and there is also the point that a ball will drop

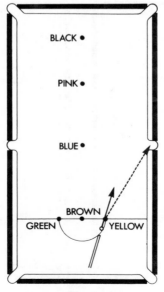

Fig. 1

into the pocket off the far jaw of the middle pocket while the near jaw tends to throw it out.

Assuming then that you have potted the yellow, your next shot will be a half-ball green, depending on the precise position in which the cue-ball finished.

The natural angle the cue-ball will take in potting the green leaves you with a choice of playing the pot slowly (Fig. 2) in order to take the brown in the opposite baulk pocket, or rather more strongly (Fig. 3) to take the brown in the same baulk pocket, or more strongly still (Fig. 4) to bounce off two cushions before taking the brown into that pocket.

The danger with the shot shown in Fig. 2 is that on many tables the cue-ball will run-off – deviate from a true course – enough to cause the shot to be missed. This is particularly likely, as with this shot, when playing across the table and slightly towards baulk.

This is because the nap of the cloth runs *from* baulk towards the top of the table. Thus, any shots which are played *against* the nap

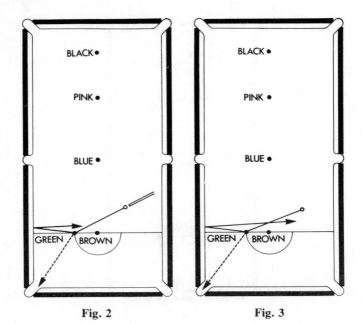

Fig. 2   Fig. 3

have a greater tendency to drift off course, as we have seen.

Figure 3 is therefore a better choice, since the cue-ball has to be hit harder and therefore has less chance to run off. Unless the table is very fast it is not all that difficult to gauge the pace of your shot to leave good position; but Fig. 4, unless the table is very slow, is, for me, a better choice still.

My own choice, though, would be none of these but the one shown in Fig. 5, which is a medium-paced stun stroke. This is because the cue-ball can be hit hard enough to avoid any possibility of it running off, and hit in such a way that it does not have to travel very far to reach its desired position on the brown.

The brown is probably the key ball in clearing the colours. The yellow, green and brown spots are all in a small area, but the blue spot is in a different part of the table. Assuming that you are playing the brown from where the cue-ball has finished in Fig. 4, you need to play a stun shot to take the cue-ball on and off the side cushion to leave an almost straight blue (see Fig. 6).

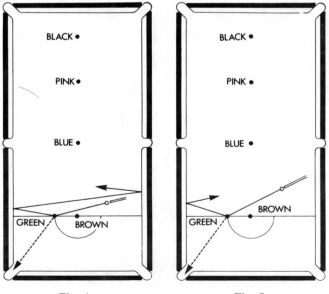

Fig. 4   Fig. 5

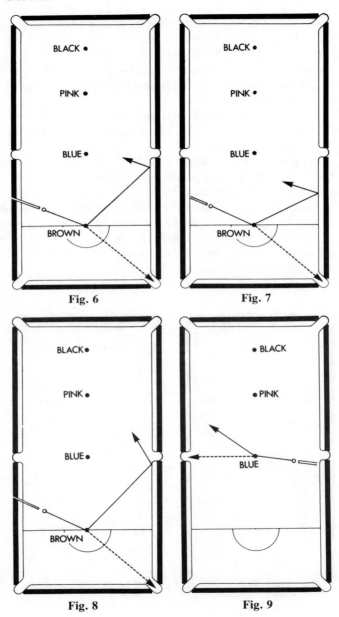

Fig. 6

Fig. 7

Fig. 8

Fig. 9

The stun shot, of course, widens the angle the cue-ball takes from the brown. Not enough stun and the blue then has to be cut into the middle pocket with a tricky positional shot for the pink (Fig. 7); too much stun and the cue-ball will go in-off in the middle pocket or go just the 'wrong' side of the blue (Fig. 8) with an even harder positional shot for the pink.

Played correctly, though, as in Fig. 6, you will leave yourself an easy blue to pot slowly for automatic good position on the pink (see Fig. 9).

If, though, you have finished too short on the blue, there are two alternatives: (*a*) to play the cut plain-ball, just missing the corner pocket, and using top and side cushions to bounce into position for the pink (see Fig. 10); or (*b*) as Fig. 11 shows (particularly if there is a danger of going in-off in the corner pocket), a stun with a little right-hand side, keeping the cue-ball nicely in the middle of the table.

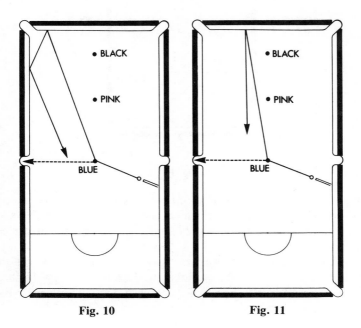

Fig. 10   **Fig. 11**

Figure 12 is a much harder positional shot for the pink, particularly if the table or cushions are on the slow side. Play with top and
left-hand side and plenty of controlled power to bring the cue-ball
off three cushions, as shown. The main difficulty with this shot is to
get the correct speed. As the cue-ball is travelling across the face of
the pink, slightly too little pace or slightly too much is going to leave
an awkward position on the pink.

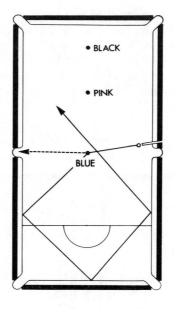

Fig. 12

Figure 13 shows one position in which the cue-ball may stop –
dead straight on the pink – in which case you play a plain-ball shot
with sufficient strength for the cue-ball to run through for perfect
position on the black.

Figure 14 shows the straightforward pot and bounce off the
cushion if the cue-ball finishes slightly to the left of a straight pot for
the pink, and Fig. 15 shows the stun shot needed if the cue-ball
finished slightly to the right of straight of the pink.

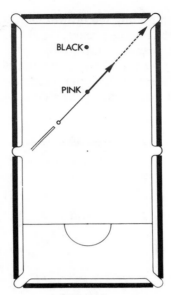

Fig. 13

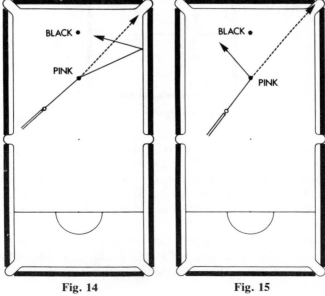

Fig. 14   Fig. 15

If the cue-ball, in potting the brown, has travelled even further
the wrong side of the middle pocket, Fig. 16 shows two alternative
methods of getting position on the pink.

You can either play plain ball off the bottom and side cushion
(shot 1) or, should the bottom corner pocket rule out this shot, with
stun and left-hand side avoiding the side cushion (shot 2, dotted
line).

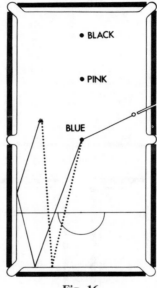

Fig. 16

Clearing the colours therefore makes you use quite a range of
positional shots – a much wider range, in fact, than just the
sequence of shots shown so far. It is good practice to attempt to
clear the colours several times if you have a few minutes to yourself,
as you will find that you will very rarely clear them with exactly the
same sequence of shots.

For instance, you may well pot the yellow in such a way as to leave
yourself straight on the green (Fig. 17). In this case, all you have to
do is to play the pot firmly with screw to bring the cue-ball back a
few inches for the brown.

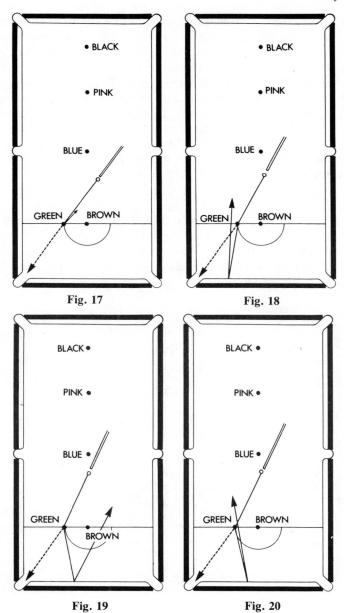

Fig. 17

Fig. 18

Fig. 19

Fig. 20

As I said earlier, potting is memory. Shot selection in positional play is largely memory as well, for only experience will enable you to recognise what path the cue-ball will take after potting a ball.

For example, there does not appear to be a great deal of difference between the angle of the pot in Figs 18, 19 and 20 but, in fact, a plain-ball shot in Fig. 19 will take the cue-ball off the bottom cushion and back onto the brown. To avoid this, play with either a little right-hand side or left-hand side, as shown.

I myself prefer left-hand side in this position since the cue-ball will gather pace after hitting the cushion instead of losing it, as it would with right-hand side.

Your position on the brown could also call for a wide range of shots. It is possible, for instance, to finish about three-quarter ball (Fig. 21) one way (so that you have to use the baulk and side cushion) or about three-quarter ball (Fig. 22) the other way (so that you have to screw back).

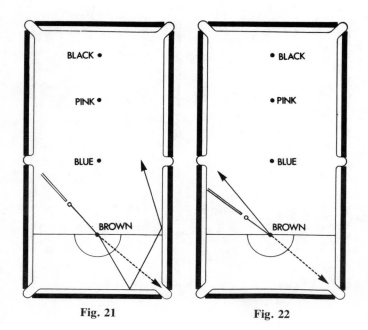

Fig. 21   Fig. 22

Figure 23 shows the half-ball pot when only one cushion is used. This is not one of my favourites, as the rest is needed to play it. Figure 24, however, which is exactly the same half-ball pot from the other side of the table, is much easier, though I myself would play this with stun as shown.

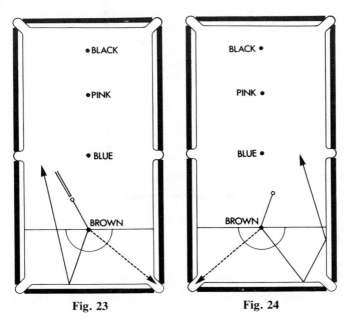

Fig. 23   **Fig. 24**

The cue-ball may stop in a number of positions on the blue, as I have already discussed in Figs 9–12 and 16, but an additional variation is Fig. 25, where the black prevents the pink being potted into the top-right pocket and where you should use screw with right-hand side, swinging the cue-ball off two cushions with running side.

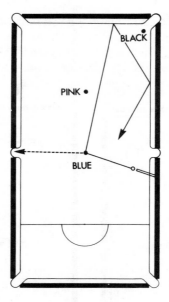

Fig. 25

Just as it is relatively easy to keep position in potting the baulk colours (yellow, green, brown) because their spots are close to each other, it should not be too difficult to take pink and black after the two trickiest parts of clearing the colours (getting position on the blue from the brown and on the pink from the blue) have been overcome.

With Fig. 14, as we have already seen, the pink is almost straight and requires only a medium-paced shot to bring the cue-ball off the side cushion into perfect position on the black.

With Fig. 15 the correct shot is simply a firm stun, but with Fig. 26, in which it is necessary to play the pot with strong right-hand side, you are dealing with a tricky shot which you should avoid if you can.

In fact, if you leave yourself in this position after potting the blue you can say that you have played a bad shot. At the same time, you

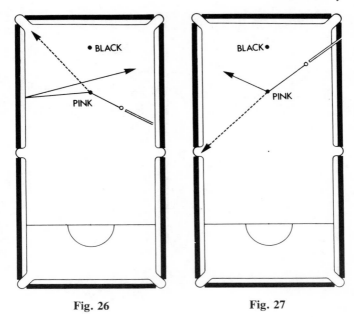

Fig. 26   **Fig. 27**

can't execute every shot as you intend, so there will be occasions when you will be forced into playing it.

Another awkward position is in Fig. 27, where the shot is to stun the pink in the middle pocket to obtain position on the black.

Many players are afraid of potting into the middle pocket at speed. It is true that bad workmanship by the table fitters can lead to a ball being potted and bouncing out of the pocket again. If I find myself on a table like this, I try to avoid this sort of shot. But on most tables you can be confident that, unless you hit the ball very, very hard, if you pot a ball it will stay potted.

If the cue-ball finishes slightly higher on the pink (Fig. 28), you are left with a plain half-ball pot, or, if it finishes slightly higher still, a thinner pot which, as Fig. 29 shows, should be played quite briskly to bring the cue-ball off three cushions, for position on the black.

Many players in this position trickle the pink towards the middle pocket but, as few tables are completely true and shots against the nap (i.e. towards the bottom cushion) almost always drift a little, I prefer to use a little more speed when possible.

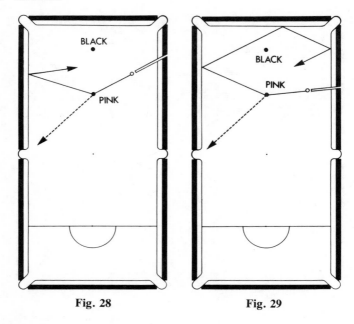

Fig. 28   **Fig. 29**

Figure 30 shows a position where no amount of check (left-hand) side is of any positional use, so there is nothing for it but to pot the pink at fair speed with screw and right-hand side to come round the table for the black off three cushions. This is a tricky shot by any standards. The most common fault is to use too much power, so that the cue-ball is forced into the jaws of the middle pocket before the screw has had time to take effect.

I myself try to let right-hand side do as much of the work as possible. This running side has the effect of adding pace to the cue-ball off the cushions.

One final way of clearing the colours, a real test of skill even for a professional, is to take them without the cue-ball touching a cushion. The secret is to finish almost straight on each ball, as Figs 31–6 show. If you can do this two or three times out of five, you should be thinking of entering the Amateur Championship!

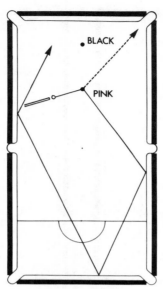

Fig. 30

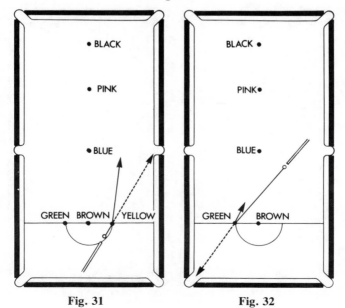

Fig. 31   **Fig. 32**

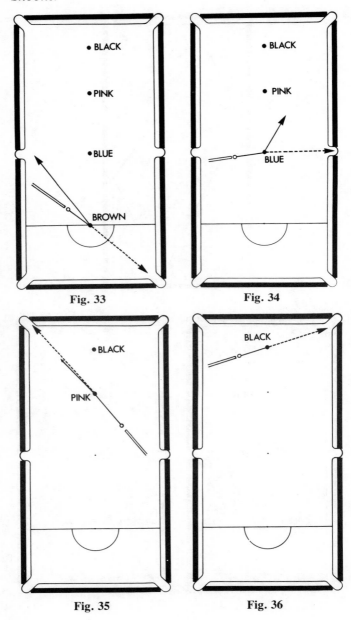

Fig. 33

Fig. 34

Fig. 35

Fig. 36

When you have mastered all these variations of clearing the colours you can consider that you have the basic equipment to cope with virtually any game situation. The only warning to add is that the colours stage of a frame removes more of the element of choice. The next ball after the yellow *must* be the green, but the next shot after the red is any colour and the next shot after a colour is any red.

Room for manoeuvre

The successful player has to think logically to plan a sequence of shots; not to plan them rigidly but in such a way as to leave himself maximum margin of error and as much scope as possible.

In Fig. 37, for example, you have a choice between two simple straight reds into the top pockets. In either case, the cue-ball only has to run through a few inches for the black, but the shot into the right-hand pocket is much the better shot because in potting it the two other reds become pottable into the opposite corner pocket later in the break.

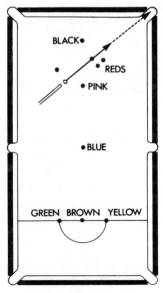

Fig. 37

The same principle applies in Fig. 38 where you have a choice of two pottable reds with three more open round the pink spot. It is easy to get on the black from the red nearer the side cushion, but the shot I would take is the one marked, because as long as that red remains on the table the black can be potted into only one of the top pockets.

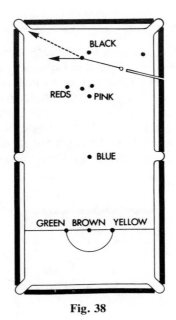

Fig. 38

Similarly, if I get a chance, I am always keen to clear any reds round the black spot which restrict my freedom of choice in the way I pot the black. For example, in Fig. 39, the red behind the black spot is so positioned that it could hamper my use of the top cushion for positional play later in the break.

Therefore, in potting the simple red to get on the black, I make sure the cue-ball stops soon enough to leave an angle on the black to lay a short screw back to take the red just behind the black spot next. The reason for this is that the red behind the black spot is making it difficult to play a positional shot or any of the other four reds if I need to use the top cushion.

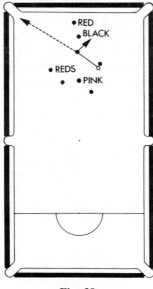

Fig. 39

Although this might be called advanced positional play, it is important to develop the mental attitude of attempting to win frames with decisive breaks, rather than waiting for opponents' errors which may never come. A lot of players are quite successful in local leagues with a policy of taking a red and a colour and then playing safe, and there are times when the position of the balls or different conditions make this necessary even at higher levels of competition. But generally a player with such a limited game is very unlikely to beat a good amateur and is unlikely ever to make much progress.

One theory I have is that a player playing the wrong shot and getting it will never improve, as he will invariably carry on playing the wrong shot throughout his career; whereas a player playing the correct shot and missing it could still become a professional if the pots start to go in, because he is thinking logically and has only to improve his ability to start making breaks.

Perhaps the most important ball to consider in break-building is the black, because in the early part of a frame most of the reds which become pottable are usually in the top third of the table. It is for this reason that most big breaks contain several blacks.

Generally, the best angle at which to pot the black is between half-ball and three-quarter ball. The reason for this can be seen from Fig. 40. If the cue-ball is straight on the black, then you can only run-through straight or screw back straight. Good players, by using left-hand side with screw, can widen the angle the cue-ball takes after hitting the cushion (see the dotted line), but even this variation does not increase the range of possibilities to compare with the range which exists for a three-quarter or half-ball shot.

Figure 40 shows two reds in such a position that if you are straight on the black there is no way of getting good position to pot either. The only possibilities are to play to leave a double (see p. 110) or to play a very good deep screw to bring the cue-ball off the side cushion, which is beyond the capabilities of most players (especially on a slow table) and which in any case leaves a pot which could not be called easy.

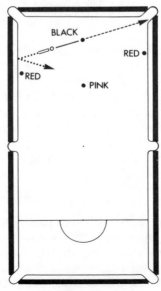

Fig. 40

Had the position been half-ball or three-quarter ball on the black it would be much easier to obtain position on either red, as you will see from the range of possibilities in Figs 41 and 42.

Figure 41 shows the variety of positions you can manoeuvre the cue-ball into from a half-ball pot.

The first possibility (shot A) is a plain-ball pot to bounce off the top cushion, gauging the strength of the shot to finish at any point along the line drawn from the top cushion. Shot B shows the pot played with strong left-hand side to spin the cue-ball off the top cushion towards the side cushion and, if necessary, away from it. A lesser degree of side would, of course, mean that the cue-ball could follow a path somewhere between the plain-ball pot and the pot with strong left-hand side. Shot C shows the stun shot without side; shot D a stun shot with right-hand side; shot E a screw shot; and shot F a screw shot with right-hand side. Finally, shot G is simply the pot with right-hand side but without stun or screw.

From this illustration it is easy to see that the cue-ball can be positioned almost anywhere in the top part of the table, according to the position of the remaining reds.

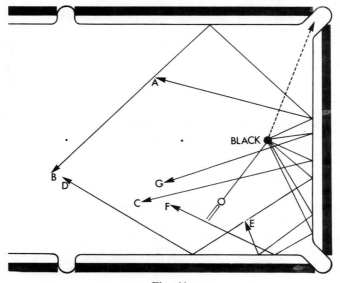

Fig. 41

Figure 42 shows the range of possibilities open for a three-quarter-ball pot.

Shot A shows what happens to the cue-ball from an ordinary run-through, while shot B shows how the cue-ball will take a wider angle from the side cushion when it carries left-hand side. Shot C is a stun shot using the top cushion – a stun run-through in effect – whereas shot D shows a slightly sharper stun striking the cue-ball slightly lower. Shot E is a stun with right-hand side, shot F a screw and shot G a slightly less deeply struck screw with right-hand side.

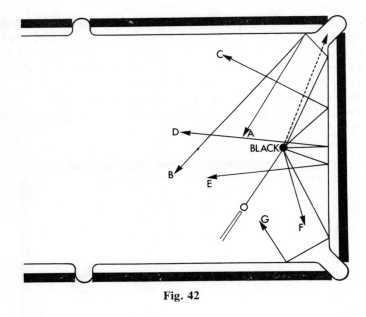

Fig. 42

Although the pink counts only one less than the black, it tends to be potted much less frequently. It starts the frame as near as possible to the apex red in the triangle without actually touching it and, in the early stages of a frame, the reds tend to spray out in such a way that one or both paths from pink spot to corner pockets become blocked.

For this reason the pink is generally potted more often when the reds have thinned out a bit. From its spot, the pink can be potted either into the top or middle pockets or even at times the baulk pockets.

As with the black, a straight pot limits the range of positions into which one can manoeuvre the cue-ball, even though the pink spot, because it is more in the middle of the table than the black spot, leaves rather more scope for run-throughs.

Figure 43 shows the straight pot into the corner pocket. The length of the screw back is limited by the middle pocket and the length of the run-through by the corner pocket.

You can also, of course, play to stop the cue-ball dead on impact with the pink by using a stun, but should you want the cue-ball to run through only about six inches past the pink spot in potting the pink I would play a shot known as the stun run-through. To play the shot, the cue-ball needs to be struck firmly and very slightly higher than would be necessary to stop it dead (Fig. 44).

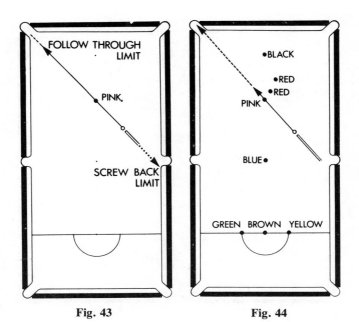

Fig. 43   Fig. 44

To do this precisely requires a sure touch and a lot of trial and error (perhaps even more than for other shots) in calculating the effect of one cloth having more or less nap than another, the liveliness of one set of balls compared with another and the relative speed of different tables.

Figure 45 shows a pot which is not straight but which nevertheless illustrates the same principle – don't play a trickle when there is any reasonable alternative.

A slow pot of the pink will leave position 1 on the red, but the more certain bet is to play the pink more firmly to bounce off the cushion to finish in position 2, which is virtually identical.

Figure 46 shows the pink being potted into the other top pocket with the cue-ball taking four possible angles from the object-ball according to the degrees of screw used, line A showing the effect when the cue-ball is struck as low as possible, line B the effect when the cue-ball is struck slightly higher, line C that when a stun stroke is used and line D the natural angle.

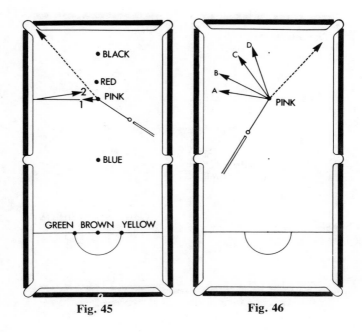

Fig. 45   Fig. 46

The same variation could be used when the cue-ball pots the pink at a similar angle from the other side of the table, though with the important difference that the shot from this side of the table would require any right-handed player either to use the rest or overstretch. This illustrates why it is safer for right-handers, if they have a choice, to pot the pink from the left-hand side of the table.

It seems comparatively dull to list all these variations in textbook isolation, but it is a lot more interesting when you have to assess the position of all the relevant balls and choose the best shot to play.

The pockets
The crucial shot in many breaks is a pot into a middle pocket, either the pink from its spot or a red from near the pink spot.

For example, Fig. 47 shows only one red left and only one way of getting position to pot it – by stunning the pink into the middle pocket.

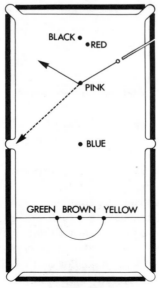

Fig. 47

A lot of players have more trouble potting into the middle pockets than into the corner pockets. I have never been conscious of this myself, but the theorists tell me that the eyes focus more naturally on two lines converging (like a corner pocket) than a point on one line (like a middle pocket).

This difficulty seems to be increased when potting into a partially 'closed' pocket (Fig. 48).

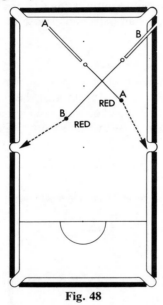

Fig. 48

Middle pockets are cut in such a way that when potting into even a slightly closed pocket the ball will only rarely enter the pocket after touching the near jaw.

Generally speaking, when the middle pocket is partially closed, it is better to aim onto the far jaw of the pocket rather than the pocket itself. If you can get just more than half a ball over the edge of the pocket, the other part, having struck the inside of the jaw, will throw the ball into the pocket rather than away from it.

This thinking is also supported by the fact that the nap of the cloth pushes the ball towards the near jaw on this kind of shot.

Figure 49 shows what should happen to this kind of pot when it is played just hard enough to reach the pocket. The ball starts out

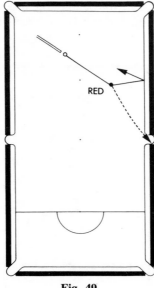

Fig. 49

bang on line for the pocket but, as it slows down, the nap forces it to drift off line and ultimately it strikes the near jaw. For this reason, when you are forced to play a slow pot against the nap into a middle pocket, aim for the far jaw of the pocket and (you hope) watch the ball curl in.

The amount of nap and therefore its strength varies from table to table. Cloths which have been on for three or four years usually have very little nap left and therefore less allowance has to be made. On the other hand, new cloths have a strong nap, and new cloths which are coarser than the best quality have the strongest nap of all. These days, high-quality championship cloths have very little nap, so very little allowance needs to be made even with the slowest of pots against the nap.

It isn't always possible to retain position on the pink and black, so it is often good policy to use the blue to keep the break going. When the remaining reds are in the top part of the table, the best angle at which to pot the blue is about three-quarter ball, because this angle gives you the greatest scope in playing your next positional shot.

In Fig. 50, for instance, you can pot the blue slowly to get red A, bounce off the cushion for red B, bounce off the cushion with left-hand side for red C, or use a screw shot to get position on red D.

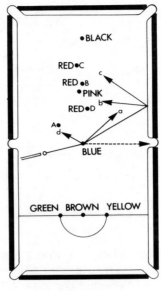

Fig. 50

In a game situation you may not have quite as many choices as this, but the general principle of getting slightly baulk-side of the blue remains. The more thinly you have to pot the blue, the more your range of positional possibilities decreases.

The thinner you contact the object-ball, the less possible it is to screw back. The thinner the object-ball is contacted, the more speed remains on the cue-ball after contact, thus further reducing the number of positions into which the cue-ball can be manoeuvred.

There are, of course, exceptions to every generalisation.

There will be times, either because it is impossible to do so or because you have not played the shot as well as you might have done, when you will finish the 'wrong' side of the blue. In other words, when the cue-ball has to travel in and out of baulk to obtain position on the next red.

Figures 12 and 16 in this chapter have already shown three ways of taking the cue-ball in and out of baulk from the blue to position on the pink, but the situation is, of course, more complicated when contact with the baulk colours, the yellow, green and brown, has to be avoided.

Figure 51 shows the cue-ball in a position on the blue where there is a considerable risk of it kissing the brown or yellow as it comes round the table. This is a risk even for a player whose knowledge of cushion angles is very good. It may still be the shot to play if, for example, either the brown or yellow or, better still, both were not on their own spots, as this would much reduce the risk of the kiss.

Otherwise, however, the better alternative is the stun with check (in this case right-hand) side.

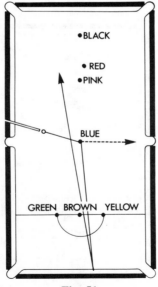

Fig. 51

Play to the cue-ball between yellow and brown slightly nearer the yellow than the brown. The right-hand side should then check the cue-ball as it strikes the baulk cushion, to a degree which enables it to return out of baulk on almost exactly the same line it has entered it.

If the cue-ball enters baulk nearer the brown than the yellow, the check side is likely to cause a collision with the brown on the return journey.

Figure 52 shows the cue-ball at exactly the same angle on the blue but the remaining pottable reds are so distributed that the 'in and out of baulk with check side' shot described for Fig. 51 is much less likely to yield good results than by playing with left-hand side, as shown. Most players find this more difficult, possibly because the left-hand side is spinning into the object-ball rather than away from it as would be the case with right-hand side. In terms of avoiding a kiss on the cue-ball's journey out of baulk, it does not much matter whether the cue-ball enters baulk nearer the brown or yellow, since the side spin will swing it off the baulk cushion between the yellow and side cushion.

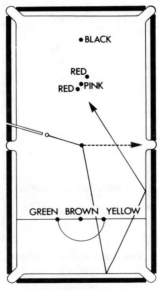

Fig. 52

Break-building

Opening the pack

At top level, break-building can be relatively easy if there are a lot of balls in obviously pottable positions. A player's extra class therefore often shows itself in the skill with which he can dislodge reds (or colours) from unpottable into pottable positions.

Figure 53 shows this at its crudest. There is no problem about potting the black, but the only way to continue the break with another red is to stun the cue-ball into the pack of reds at speed and trust to luck. You can reduce the odds a little in your favour by going into the edge of the pack (see arrow) rather than the middle, but even so the final position of the balls and your chances of continuing the break are largely a matter of luck.

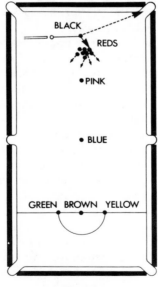

Fig. 53

Generally, the tighter the bunch of reds is packed together the less chance you will have of opening them up successfully, since the cue-ball, unless it strikes the pack a glancing blow (and sometimes not even then), will very often finish in the middle of the pack, perhaps even touching a red, and therefore in no position to pot anything.

Sometimes, however, it is possible to plan a little further ahead by loosening the pack slightly two shots in advance.

In Fig. 54 the obvious, indeed only, shot is to pot the black and stun off the top cushion for the only loose red. What is not so obvious is the precise position in which you should aim to leave the cue-ball in relation to this red.

If you leave a dead straight pot you will be able to run through for the black again, or if the cue-ball travels slightly further you will be able to play a soft screw to hold position on the black.

The snag in both cases is that the cue-ball eventually has to go into a tight pack, so the better alternative would be to leave the cue-ball slightly short on the loose red so that you can pot it with screw and right-hand side and use the side of the pack to take the cue-ball down the table for the blue (see Fig. 55).

In doing this you are certain to retain position on the blue and dislodge some reds from the pack. It is quite likely that you will then be able to play a positional shot from the blue onto a loose red but, even if this is not possible, the pack will have become loosened enough to increase your chances of cannoning into it in such a way as to leave some reds pottable.

Figure 56 offers a similar opportunity, though this time by using the back of the pack instead of the side. The art of the shot, once more, is not to leave yourself straight on the loose red but at an angle, to enable the cue-ball to cannon off the back reds into position on the black while at the same time loosening the pack.

Figure 57 is a development of this shot. In this position, the plain-ball pot will mean that the cue-ball will not strike the pack, so to achieve this it is necessary to screw into the end red as shown. The secret is to catch the further half of the end red so that the cue-ball flicks away from it to leave a good angle for potting the black. The common message from Figs 54–7 is that it is better to avoid going into the pack with a view to playing a ball from the pack next shot, in favour of preparing the way one or two shots *in advance*.

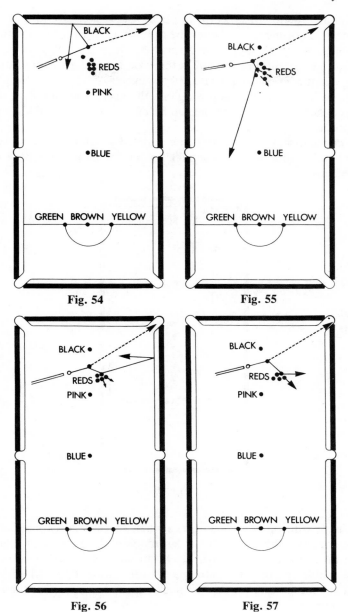

Fig. 54

Fig. 55

Fig. 56

Fig. 57

In Fig. 58, for instance, the greenest beginner would have no trouble in potting the red over the right-hand top pocket, followed by the pink over the opposite top pocket. The pack could, of course, be opened off either ball, but in this case I would attempt to open the pack three shots in advance by potting another red past the pink into the top pocket and screwing into the pack. The pink is so near the pocket that, wherever the cue-ball finishes, you should be able to pot it.

This, in turn, will leave the other easy red over the top pocket and a 'second chance' to open the pack if your first try is not completely satisfactory.

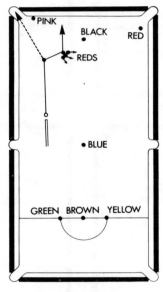

Fig. 58

There will, of course, be times when there is no choice but to leave opening the pack until the last moment. In these cases, all you can do is to make sure you leave an angle on the black which will enable you to get into the pack easily (about half-ball is ideal) and to aim for that part of the pack which seems to offer the best possibilities.

For example, better results are usually achieved by taking the cue-ball *inside* the cluster of reds rather than hitting the *outside* of the cluster. In Fig. 59 – a simple instance – you will be virtually certain to finish in a good position if you can, in potting the black, take the cue-ball on the path arrowed between the outer reds. However, if the cue-ball should strike either of these reds the chances of continuing your break are negligible.

The black is not always the best ball from which to break the pack. In Fig. 60 you have the chance of potting the loose red and running through for the black. It would then be possible to go into the pack from the black, but there are a couple of things which could go wrong.

First, you could contact the solidly packed back four reds and leave the cue-ball in the middle of them without a hope of potting a red or, second, in attempting to catch the side of the pack you might miss the pack altogether. Both these dangers are increased by the cue-ball having some distance to travel before contacting the reds.

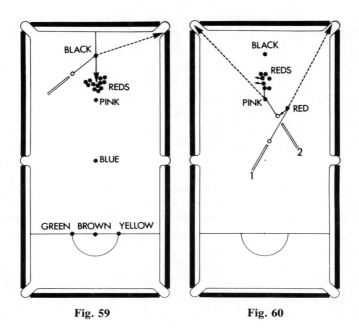

Fig. 59   Fig. 60

This illustrates the advantage of not running through for the black but of screwing back a couple of inches for the pink. Any angle on the pink from almost straight to half-ball means not only that the cue-ball will be bound to kiss the reds but that it will also knock them in the general direction of the top pocket.

When playing a cannon at billiards it is invariably easier to play a precise contact onto the second object-ball if this is near the first object-ball than it is if they are some distance apart. This is even more true at snooker when the first object-ball has to be potted, and is an important factor in a position like this in choosing to play for the pink rather than the black.

One ball with which many players choose to split the pack is the blue, but this yields good position less frequently than one might expect. The main snag about the blue is the natural triangle shape of the reds. Very often a few reds are detached and potted but halfway through a frame seven or eight remain at the core of the original triangle still in more or less the original triangular shape.

This means that if the cue-ball contacts this triangular shape from the direction of the blue spot it will tend to bounce off the red towards or even into one of the corner pockets.

There are times, of course, when the balls break open nicely from this shot, but whenever I am forced into playing it I am never surprised when the cue-ball finishes somewhere near the jaws of the corner pocket with only an awkward cut back into the opposite top pocket to go for next (see Fig. 61).

I therefore prefer, when it is possible, to leave an angle on the blue which will enable me to use the side and top cushion to go into the pack diagonally from the back (see Fig. 62).

The pack can also be split from the spotted yellow, green or brown, or indeed from any colour which is not on its spot. Often the cue-ball may be in such a position that you could easily pot any of the three baulk colours. In this case, your choice of shot depends on the exact shape of the pack.

In Fig. 63, for instance, I could pot the green and screw off the side cushion with right-hand side towards the pack of reds. As the green is a three-quarter-ball pot, I would have to hit the cue-ball very hard with just the right degree of screw and side. Too much or

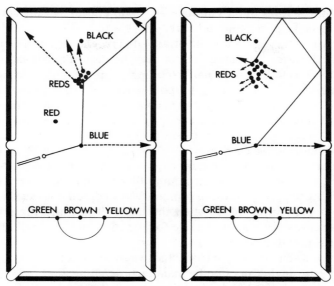

Fig. 61   Fig. 62

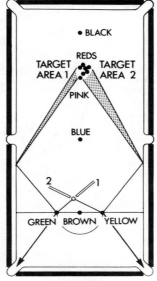

Fig. 63

too little screw (and it's all too easy to do either) and the cue-ball will miss the pack. End of break.

It would therefore be more sensible to take the yellow. The pot is half-ball instead of three-quarter and therefore the cue-ball does not have to be struck so hard to propel it up the table, hitting the cushion with left-hand side, to split the reds. You can also see from the diagram that the target area of the pack is greater from the yellow than it is from the green.

Clearing from the cushion
Similar skills to those required for opening a pack of reds are needed to dislodge reds or colours which lie on or near a cushion.

Figure 64, in fact, shows a common way of dislodging a cushioned red in potting the blue, when the half-ball pot into the middle pocket provides a natural angle for the cue-ball to bounce off the top cushion to contact the red.

Even when the cannon from blue to cushion is not quite a natural angle, the angle can often be manufactured quite easily by using a little right- or left-hand side, as the case may be.

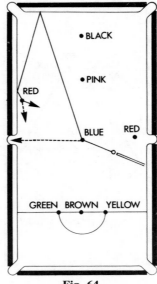

Fig. 64

When dislodging a cushioned red, it is always handy to have an 'open' red in reserve. In Fig. 64, there is an open red near the pocket. Most players would simply pot the blue, take the easy red, another blue and only then start thinking about the cushioned red, whereas with logical thinking the shot to play is to pot the blue and attempt to move the cushioned red. If you fail to make the cannon, the easy red will still be pottable, provided you play at a speed to leave the cue-ball between the blue spot and the baulk line. If the cannon is successful the cushioned red should become pottable and you should be able to compile a frame-winning break.

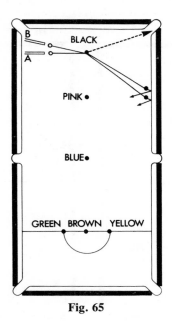

Fig. 65

Figure 65 shows a common method of disturbing a red on the side cushion by potting the black. The secret of this shot is obtaining precise position on the black.

From position A, the pot allows a natural cannon onto the baulk-side red, whereas the cue-ball needs to be slightly nearer the top cushion to allow a natural cannon onto the other red.

This type of shot should not be played at more than medium speed, as you do not want to put much distance between the cue-ball and the second object-ball once the cannon has been made.

Figure 66 shows a much more difficult position from which to cannon the red into the open, as a stun stroke has to be used to make the cannon.

It is not all that easy to make the cannon and there is a possibility that the cue-ball will strike the red full or nearly full so that a double-kiss takes place and the red remains where it is. Quite frankly, some luck is needed to contact the red on either side from this shot and even then it is not certain to go into an easily pottable position.

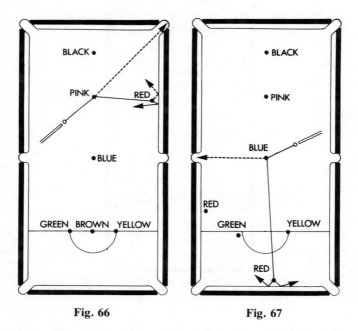

Fig. 66   Fig. 67

Figure 67 shows a position from which it is even more unlikely that you will make a completely successful cannon.

However, the cannon is still worth trying at moderate pace so that you can then put your opponent in trouble with a safety shot if your original intention does not work out.

4

Safety Play

There are two types of safety play, positive and negative. The object of positive safety is to make your opponent's next shot so difficult that he is almost bound to give you a good opening. The object of negative safety is merely to prevent your opponent from scoring.

The most aggressive form of safety is the snooker, thus compelling your opponent either to play a swerve shot or to use one or more cushions. The next best form of safety is a shot which leaves the cue-ball tight against a cushion and the object-ball some distance away and not over a pocket.

Aggressive safety is a means of remaining in tactical control of a frame, but it is always good to remember that, in the end, you have to pot balls to win. In other words, safety play and snookering can only be means to an end.

It is also as well to remember that, while prolonged bouts of safety play can disturb your opponent's confidence and potting rhythm, they can also disturb your own rhythm.

Since I turned professional my own game has become more and more aggressive, partly because I have gained in confidence through my successes and partly because in playing good players you have to win through your own good play rather than wait for mistakes which never come.

Most readers of this book will be a long way below professional standard, but even then my advice is to be as aggressive as you can within the limits of your ability, by taking chances which are fair risks rather than stupid gambles.

As long as you think aggressively and positively, you are mentally attuned to winning, whereas if you continually think defensively you are merely trying to avoid defeat.

In many matches, the mental balance changes, often several times. Given an identical shot, there may be a time to attack and a time to defend, although there are certain shots which should be attempted (or not attempted) regardless of the state of the frame.

Ideally, the best shots to play are those which offer the maximum possible benefit for the least risk, which is a good business principle, and the worst shots those which offer the least potential benefit but the maximum risk. The idea is, with clear thinking and good concentration, to play shots in the first category yourself and force your opponent to play plenty of shots in the second.

Breaking-off

You can start controlling the tactical pattern of a frame with your very first shot, the break-off.

There are three variants of this, in each of which the main principle is to place the cue-ball as near as possible to the baulk cushion.

With shot 1 (Fig. 1), place the cue-ball about four inches from the yellow and play to hit the outside red quarter-ball with right-hand side and sufficient strength to bring the cue-ball off three cushions to rest on the baulk cushion below the green.

With this shot you can be virtually certain of not leaving a potting chance, and can possibly leave your opponent snookered or with an awkward thin safety shot as he himself attempts to return the cue-ball to the baulk cushion.

Even if your opponent, with his first shot, manages to deny you a good opening, he may have had to devote so much of his concentration to this that he cannot really attempt to land you in trouble as well.

The snag with shots which disturb the pack of reds is that one or two reds can go near enough to a pocket for your opponent to be tempted into potting one.

This snag applies to shot 2 (Fig. 2), a similar break-off to shot 1 except that the outside red in the back row but one is struck quarter-ball with running side.

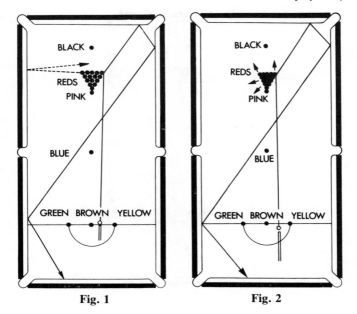

Fig. 1   Fig. 2

This break-off disturbs the last *two* rows of reds while the break-off in shot 1 disturbs only the back row to any significant degree.

Shot 2, played perfectly, will land your opponent in more difficulty than shot 1, but shot 2, played slightly wrong, is more likely to give your opponent a reasonable opening.

If, for instance, you contact the red at less than a quarter-ball, the cue-ball will cannon into the end red, remain in the top part of the table and almost certainly leave your opponent a good opening.

Then again, if you contact the red at more than a quarter-ball, the cue-ball will spring off wider and either hit the jaws of the corner pocket or actually go in-off.

On a strange table, particularly one with a strong nap, shot 2 is much more risky than shot 1. On the other hand, if you are confident and believe that opening up the reds as soon as possible is to your advantage, then consider shot 2.

Shot 3, a break-off which some players favour, consists of striking the end red and bringing the cue-ball back to the baulk cushion off

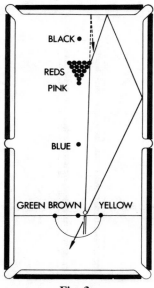

Fig. 3

only two cushions, as shown in Fig. 3.

One obvious snag about this is that there is not much space between yellow and brown for the cue-ball to reach the baulk cushion, whereas in shots 1 and 2, once the cue-ball has got past the blue, there is a much wider margin of error in bringing it to the baulk cushion from between the yellow and the side cushion.

A kiss on the brown is therefore quite likely to give your opponent a potting chance or the opportunity to put you on the baulk cushion.

To sum up, shot 1 is probably the most reliable break-off, with shot 2 a good one to introduce if you want to put a greater emphasis on attack. Sometimes, it is also worth breaking-off with the cue-ball between the green and brown rather than the brown and yellow, as some players can more consistently hit the left of an object-ball in a safety shot than the right.

Most frames start with an exchange of safety shots which is ended either by a player taking a risk, making a mistake or potting a 'shot to nothing'.

Shots to nothing

Shots to nothing, as their name implies, offer a chance of a pot with little or no risk of leaving a pot for one's opponent if the pot is missed, but unless you are fortunate enough to be left a position in which one of these is 'on', you will have to rely on forcing an opening through one of several types of orthodox safety shots.

The secret of many safety shots is simply hitting the object-ball thin. Thin contacts mean that the cue-ball will carry much more speed than the object-ball and therefore, unless other balls are contacted, the cue-ball will travel much further than the object-ball.

In Fig. 4, the thin safety shot shown should, with the right strength, leave the cue-ball on the baulk cushion behind the green at the same time cutting the red into the pack. If the pack was not there, you would have to consider the danger of leaving the red over the top pocket and would probably have to decide to play another shot.

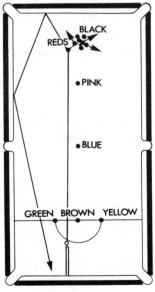

Fig. 4

In Fig. 5, there is no possibility of an in-off, but it is very important to make a thin contact to produce the successful safety shot shown, as there are particular problems in playing safe off a ball which is only an inch or so off the cushion.

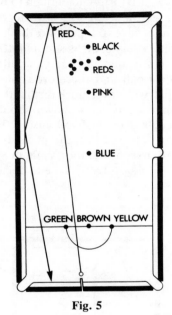

Fig. 5

The cue-ball, after striking the object-ball, springs away from the object-ball as shown in Fig. 6, before curving back onto a straight line.

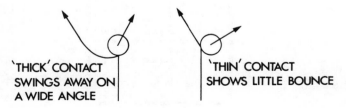

Fig. 6

Therefore, if the cue-ball has not 'straightened out' before it strikes the cushion it will obviously leave the cushion at a wider angle than if it had already straightened out.

The significance of this is that if you do catch the red thick (see Fig. 7) the cue-ball will remain in the top part of the table and almost certainly leave your opponent a good opening.

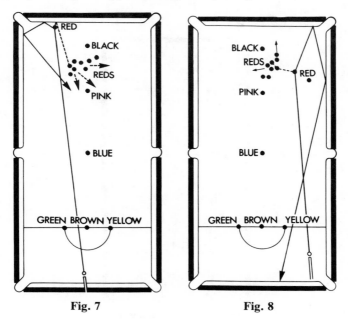

Fig. 7   Fig. 8

Another useful thin safety shot is the one shown in Fig. 8. There is some danger of an in-off in the top pocket if you catch the red too thick, but if you contact the red very thin as shown you can turn what at first glance looks like an awkward position to your own advantage.

One advanced safety shot in which a thin contact is essential is shown in Fig. 9. A plain-ball thin safety shot will take the cue-ball into the cluster near the side cushion, but if the shot is played with strong right-hand (check) side, the cue-ball will return down the table along the 'corridor' between this and the other three-ball cluster which is free of any obstructing balls.

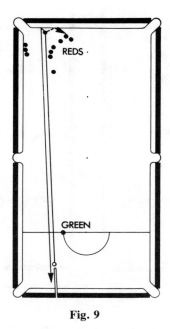

Fig. 9

Figure 10 shows a straightforward way of getting back to the baulk cushion by using the top cushion, and Figs 11 and 12 two ways of getting back by using side with about a quarter-ball contact.

In Fig. 11, right-hand side is used to check the cue-ball off the top and side cushions to avoid kissing the balls lying between the pink spot and the side cushion, while Fig. 12 shows how you will need left-hand side to avoid kissing the reds near the side cushion.

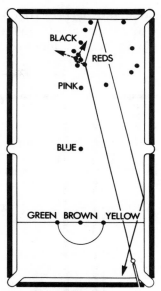

Fig. 10

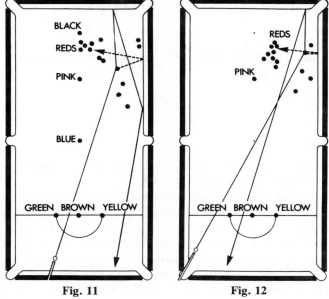

Fig. 11   Fig. 12

Figure 13 shows another use of check (right-hand) side in safety play, while Fig. 14 shows a means of using right-hand (running) side to put the cue-ball under the baulk cushion in loosening out the pack of reds.

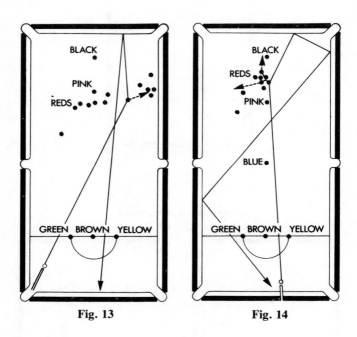

Fig. 13   **Fig. 14**

Shots to nothing cannot really go wrong, but it is very important to play them with a positive approach.

Just as some players get over-tense in playing pots which are certain to leave a good opening if they are missed, so some players do not concentrate enough on the pot in a shot to nothing if they have the consolation at the back of their minds that no immediate harm will befall them if they miss.

But in a frame of snooker I usually find that if a player misses chances early on, things usually run against him towards the end.

In Fig. 15, for instance, the reds have been disturbed in the initial safety exchange and the baulk colours have been dislodged from their spots.

There is a possible chance of potting the indicated red without the cue-ball cannoning into the other reds. Your basic knowledge of angles will tell you that if the red is struck about half-ball, the cue-ball will follow the path shown, finishing behind the green and brown.

If the red is struck slightly more or slightly less than half-ball it will not be potted, but the cue-ball will follow roughly the same path, still leaving your opponent behind the green and brown.

If the ball is potted, the yellow is available near the baulk pocket to continue your break.

There are many other examples of a shot to nothing. One of the most common is the red which seems at first glance to be in the main pack but is in fact half an inch or so clear, so that the safety shot to the baulk area can be combined with an attempted pot, as in Fig. 16.

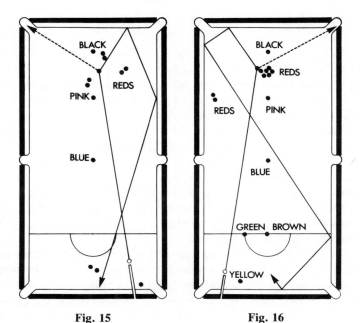

Fig. 15   **Fig. 16**

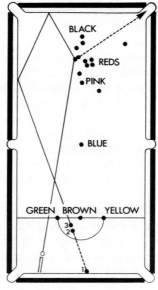

Fig. 17

Another shot to nothing to look for is the plant or set. There is a lot to learn about plants and sets (see p. 115), but Fig. 17 shows a simple plant, knocking one red onto another red to send the latter into the pocket. As long as the cue-ball contacts the first red about quarter-ball, this should be quite easy.

In contrast to Figs 15 and 16, I have assumed in Fig. 17 that the three baulk colours are on their spots. Therefore, assuming you pot a red, you will have a choice of either playing another pot to continue your break or playing a snooker so that your opponent not only cannot score but is likely to leave you another opening.

In the first position, for instance, the cue-ball has finished dead on the baulk cushion, so it is too risky to try to pot one of the baulk colours in a middle pocket.

The correct shot in this case is to roll the cue-ball up to the brown, contacting it as gently as possible, to leave your opponent snookered and thus likely to give you an opening.

In the second position, however, the cue-ball has come to rest away from the baulk cushion, to offer you a chance to pot the brown in the middle and take the cue-ball up the table for one of the loose reds to continue your break.

In the third position you can play the snooker or pot the brown, but this time the angle is not such that you can take the cue-ball up the table.

In this case, the shot you choose to play depends very much on the position of the reds. If there are several in the open and your opponent is going to need a lot of skill and luck to avoid giving you an opening, then a snooker is the shot.

If, on the other hand, it is comparatively easy for your opponent to avoid leaving an opening, then pot the brown and make your following safety shot as good as possible.

Playing to the cushion

One of the secrets of good safety play is bringing the cue-ball back as near as possible to the baulk cushion. Conversely, another secret is preventing your opponent from doing so.

In Fig. 18, for instance, the shot seems to be a straightforward thin contact on the reds and a return to the baulk cushion, thus giving your opponent a chance to make a similar reply.

However, the correct shot is much more positive. Notice the position of the brown and the blue, and consider that it is impossible for your opponent to play an orthodox return to baulk from anywhere in baulk to the right of the brown spot.

Therefore, the correct shot is to contact the red as shown, with strong left-hand side to swing the cue-ball round off three cushions, to leave it on the baulk cushion for your opponent with no hope of his making a similar reply.

Figure 19 shows another position in which it is impossible to make a return to the baulk cushion. You could, of course, simply roll up to the pack of reds, but this negative shot would only allow your opponent to play thinly off the pack to leave you on the baulk cushion once again.

So the shot I would play would be to contact the red almost full-ball, as shown, to send it off the top cushion and into baulk while the cue-ball bounces off the side cushion to rest on the top cushion.

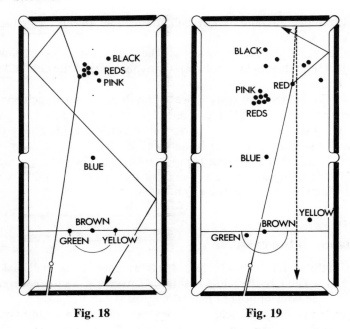

Fig. 18   **Fig. 19**

Because the cushion prevents your opponent from hitting the cue-ball low enough to get it back to the top cushion, he is going to have a difficult task leaving you safe, particularly since the red you have sent down into baulk rules out an orthodox safety shot to the baulk cushion.

Often, of course, you won't be able to get out of trouble and put your opponent in trouble quite as neatly as that. In a safety exchange, it is more usual for one player to look on top, the other to neutralise the advantage and then perhaps, a shot or two later, gain the upper hand himself.

Which shot to play?

One point to remember is that it is sometimes as unwise to be over-ambitious with a safety shot as it is with a pot.

Figure 20a, for instance, shows a possible return to the baulk

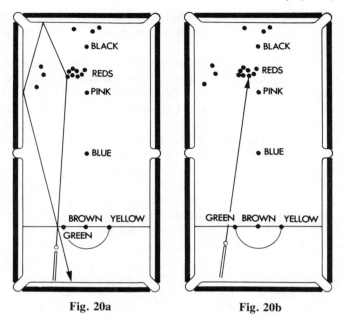

Fig. 20a   **Fig. 20b**

cushion which demands very good judgment of cushion angles to avoid cannoning on the red near the side cushion. This is the sort of shot which is more quickly mastered by players who have played some billiards than those who have not, the theory being that if billiards players have had some practice in getting cushion cannons they will be better equipped to avoid cannons in a frame of snooker.

Figure 20b shows exactly the same position except that the important red is slightly nearer the cushion and therefore makes the return to the baulk cushion much too risky.

In this case, the shot to play is a 'containing' type of safety shot, in other words one from which you don't expect to gain much immediate advantage but which, at the same time, will not present your opponent with an immediate opening. He will, at least, have to play another good shot to put you in trouble.

Therefore, it is probably best to trickle the cue-ball up to the pack (as shown), unless you are feeling confident enough to have a go at the difficult but pottable red up the side cushion.

Just as a chess player works towards his objective through a series of moves, a snooker player can plan to trap his opponent some shots in advance.

One of the most frequent examples of this is when there is one or more reds down the table and a 'top cushion' safety duel is taking place with the reds which are in the top part of the table (Fig. 21a).

In these duels, the object is to force your opponent into being first to play down the table. If there are two reds near the side cushion, as shown, and it is your shot, it is important not to allow your opponent to send the other red down the table to leave you in trouble, which is exactly what will happen if you play the shot shown in Fig. 21a.

With the first red sent down the table, the second red will finish in a position to leave your opponent almost exactly the same shot you had, except that this time you are going to be stranded on the top cushion with all the reds well down the table.

To avoid leaving your opponent to play the last red in the top part of the table (see Fig. 21b), play more thinly with left-hand side so that neither red is moved very much and the cue-ball finishes on the

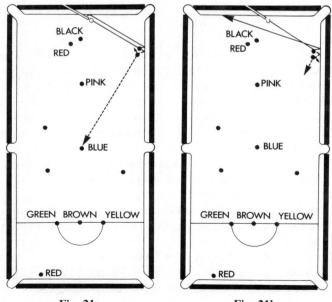

Fig. 21a   Fig. 21b

top cushion about a foot from the corner pocket. You may, in fact, snooker your opponent on these two reds behind the pink and black, but even if the pink and black were somewhere else this would still be a good tactical shot.

It is important, when you have a chance to put your opponent in trouble, that you put him in the maximum trouble.

In Fig. 22a, for instance, it is simple to play a snooker behind the green by sending the red up the table and following through a few inches with a plain-ball shot.

Figure 22b, however, shows a much more positive shot, hitting the red much harder so that it opens the pack of reds round the pink spot and stunning the cue-ball so that it remains behind the green. The advantage of this shot is that your opponent is going to be struggling to avoid giving you a chance to make a frame-winning break, as every red may now be pottable. With the other shot, of course, only one red is loose, so that even if you are left in a position to pot it (which is unlikely if your opponent keeps his head) you will still have to open the pack before continuing your break.

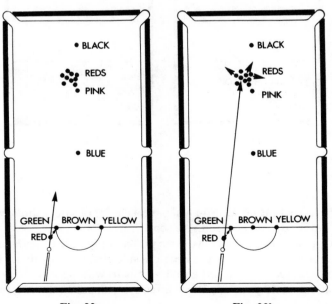

Fig. 22a   **Fig. 22b**

In Fig. 23a, some players will be so impatient to leave a snooker behind the yellow, which their opponents should have little difficulty in playing an orthodox escape as shown in shot 2, that they will overlook the much tougher snooker which can be laid behind the blue (Fig. 23b). Here the green and brown hamper the escape towards the comparative security of the pack of reds and increase the possibility of one's opponent leaving one of the open reds.

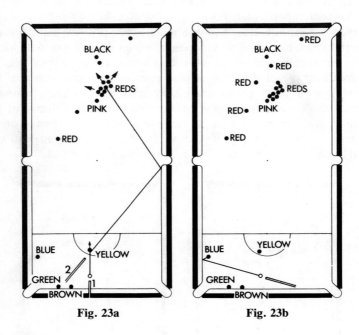

Fig. 23a   Fig. 23b

There are times when you will have a choice of safety shots, when you should decide according to score.

In Fig. 24a, for instance, you can play a safety shot either from the open red or the one which is near the side cushion. If you are 30 *in front*, you need only a red and a colour to win the frame, barring snookers, while your opponent effectively needs both reds and all the colours.

Your best tactic is therefore to play safe from the red which is already loose, as shown, the theory being that even if you lose the safety duel on this red, your opponent has still to out-manoeuvre you again to take the other red.

If, on the other hand, you are 30 *behind* in this position, play safe from the red which is near the cushion, so that both reds are in the open (see Fig. 24b). If this is so, and you can get a chance to pot one red, the odds are in your favour to take the other red as well.

You should also apply this principle in other positions towards the end of a frame. If your opponent needs all the colours to win and one or more balls is lying awkwardly near a cushion, don't cannon them into the centre of the table if you can possibly avoid it.

With all the colours pottable, you have only got to make one mistake to throw the frame away, whereas, with one or more balls under the cushion, you will almost certainly get another chance.

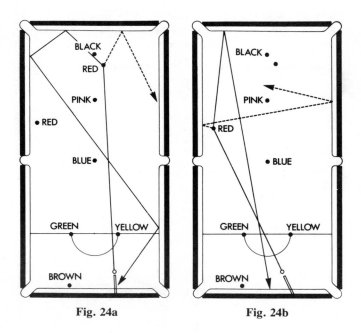

Fig. 24a   **Fig. 24b**

Safety with the colours

Safety play and snookering on the colours are arts in themselves. When there are plenty of reds on the table, the importance of snookering is entirely tactical, but at the colours stage, 4, 5, 6 or 7 penalty points can make a great deal of difference.

If you are 22 in front on the green and force your opponent to concede 4 penalty points, he cannot then win unless you concede penalty points. Even if you are only 17 in front on the green and you receive 4 penalty points, it means that you need only one ball (instead of two) to win the frame while your opponent now needs them all.

Laying snookers on the colours

There are innumerable ways in which the balls can be positioned at the colours stage, but at a reasonable standard it is quite usual to see most of the colours on their spots.

If brown, blue and pink are on their spots, it can be quite easy to leave your opponent snookered. In Fig. 25, for instance, you can play a possible but very risky double or play the shot shown which

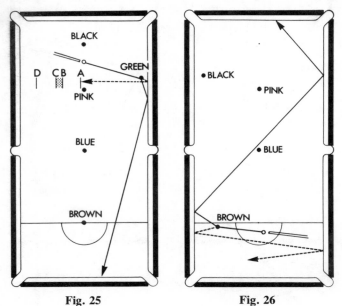

Fig. 25   Fig. 26

takes advantage of the fact that brown, blue and pink combine to screen a fairly large area into which to try to send the green.

Provided you drop the cue-ball within an inch or two of the point indicated, there is almost two feet to play with between points A and D, between pink and side cushion, to hide the green behind. The only exception is the small dotted area, CB. If the green finishes here there is a narrow path through for the cue-ball between brown and blue. The significance of this is that there is a greater chance of laying a snooker if there is more than one ball to 'hide' behind.

The same principle applies if blue and pink are on their spots (see Fig. 26), where again there is quite a wide margin of error for you to attempt to play a snooker. If, in conjunction with the snooker, you can leave the cue-ball right on the cushion, this will add to your opponent's difficulty in making an escape.

Figure 27 illustrates how green and blue can offer a similar margin of error in laying a snooker on the yellow, and Fig. 28 shows how yellow and blue can mask the last red. If the red stops anywhere in the shaded area and the cue-ball finishes on the baulk cushion, your opponent will be snookered. In the diagram it looks as if the red

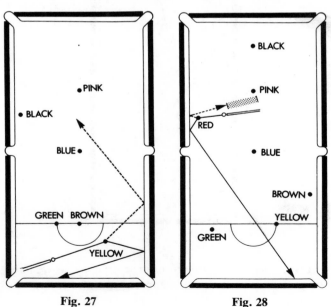

Fig. 27   Fig. 28

would be hidden only in part of this area, but the scale is misleading here as I can assure you that actually on the table the margin of error is as stated. Move the cue-ball along the baulk cushion a couple of inches either way and there is still a good margin of error in which to snooker your opponent.

Even in the early stages of a frame, it is often useful to keep these 'masking' areas in mind, either to snooker your opponent or to reduce the range of reds which he is able to hit.

One final masking area which can also be useful, particularly near the end of a frame, is that provided by pink and black, as shown in Fig. 29. This reveals only a small channel (shaded area) between pink and black through which the cue-ball could travel to hit the blue. Send the blue either side of this narrow channel and there is a very considerable area in which your opponent is bound to be snookered.

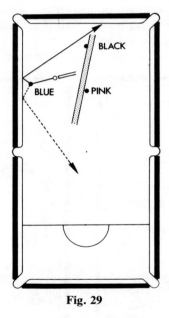

Fig. 29

Apart from the tactical functions of safety play, as we have seen, you sometimes need snookers near the end of a frame to extract penalty points before potting the last few balls to win a frame.

These snookers have to be particularly good, since you do not derive any advantage unless your opponent actually misses the ball on.

I particularly remember one snooker which was laid against me by Ray Reardon and cost me a tournament final.

Ray needed a snooker with only the pink and black left in the final frame, but played thin off the pink as shown to leave the pink in the baulk area and the cue-ball, after striking four cushions, right behind the black (Fig. 30).

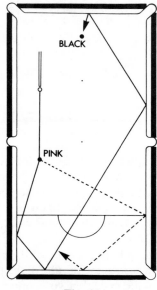

Fig. 30

This was a difficult snooker to escape from because:

(*a*) the pink was some distance away;
(*b*) the pink was far enough away from all cushions to leave plenty of room for the cue-ball to go round it;
(*c*) the cue-ball was so close to the black as to prevent me aiming a plain-ball shot at the spot on the side cushion I would have needed to hit to make a one-cushion escape.

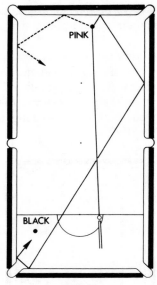

Fig. 31

Players with some experience of billiards often learn to lay these snookers more quickly than those who have only ever played snooker. In Fig. 31, with the pink near the top cushion, the cue-ball in the 'D', and the black near the baulk pocket, the position is similar to one at billiards in which you would play an all-round cannon off four cushions.

In billiards, you would hope, if you got the cannon, to leave the first object-ball somewhere in the middle of the table. But in playing snooker you would make sure that you contacted the first object-ball at less than half-ball so that your opponent would still have to play a longish shot if you fail to get the cue-ball behind the second object-ball, the black.

Therefore, play with right-hand side to swing the cue-ball round the table as shown.

There are innumerable variations of this. In Fig. 32, play thin with right-hand side to leave the pink on the baulk cushion and send the cue-ball off three cushions to finish behind the black.

In Fig. 33, play the pink about three-quarter-ball with right-hand (check) side, and in Fig. 34 thin with right-hand (running) side.

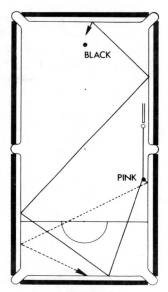

Fig. 32

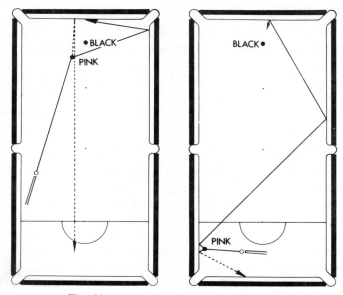

Fig. 33   **Fig. 34**

These shots are not as easy as they appear on the diagrams and your ability to play them will come only with experience. In fact, it is these tactical aspects of the game which generally catch out promising young players, rather than the more straightforward business of potting, which can largely be a matter of natural talent.

Escaping from snookers

The other side of the coin, as far as laying snookers is concerned, is escaping from them.

When your opponent cannot win the frame unless you concede penalty points, nothing really matters except hitting the ball 'on'. Some escapes can be easy, like the simple judgment of the angle a cue-ball needs to take off one cushion to hit the pink (the ball 'on'), as shown in Fig. 35.

One-cushion escapes can be more difficult if, as in Fig. 36, there is some reason why a plain-ball shot cannot be used to contact the ball 'on', the pink.

The escape in Fig. 37 is even more difficult. The middle pocket is in the way of the escape off the right-hand-side cushion, and the pink is in the way of the escape off the left-hand-side cushion.

In this case, you will need to use left-hand side to widen the angle the cue-ball takes from the side cushion to escape from the snooker, as shown.

Part of the difficulty of this shot is that the cue-ball has to take a very wide angle off the side cushion as, generally speaking, the straighter the rebound which is necessary, the easier it is to calculate.

At the risk of labouring this point, it could be said that a straight or nearly straight rebound will be the same on any table, but the angle of a wide rebound will vary considerably according to the condition of the rubber and cloth on the cushions. The more recently a cushion has been re-clothed, the wider the angle of rebounds tends to be.

Figure 38 shows an elementary two-cushion escape. Why not make the escape off one cushion? Simply because the ball 'on', the red, is bound to cannon into either green or brown if you hit it off the baulk cushion, whereas it will come clear and in all probability safe if you use the side cushion as well.

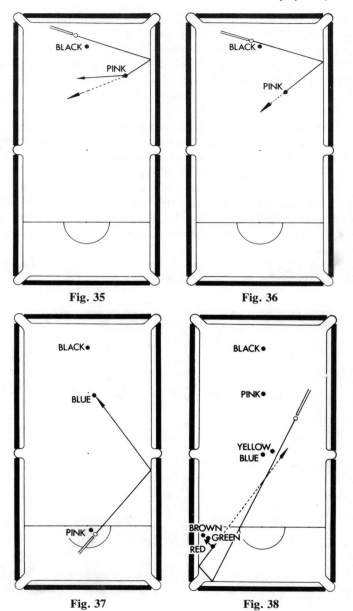

Fig. 35

Fig. 36

Fig. 37

Fig. 38

When the ball you are trying to hit is well away from the cushion, it generally pays to play with reasonable strength, thus putting some distance between cue-ball and object-ball for your opponent.

If, however, the ball you are trying to hit is near a cushion, as in Fig. 39, it generally pays to roll up to it as gently as you can, thus leaving the cue-ball so close to the object-ball that it is impossible to pot it.

In this particular position this 'slow roll' escape also leaves the cue-ball near a cushion and thus awkwardly placed to play any other red. It is likely that your opponent will snooker you again, but this at least is better than giving him a chance to make a winning break.

This principle also applies to the shot in Fig. 40, where you have a choice of two escape routes. Obviously, it is better to use the right-hand-side cushion rather than the left, because you can then play into the packed and therefore safe reds rather than towards the loose pottable reds.

Played at exactly the right weight, as shown, this escape is completely safe. Your opponent may then put you in trouble again,

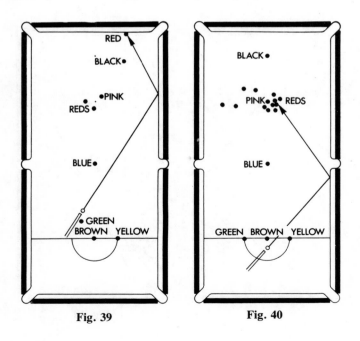

Fig. 39   Fig. 40

but will require a good shot to do so. In any case, you will have gained some breathing space.

Finally, there are occasions when the balls are so placed that you cannot use the cushions, but instead have to rely on a swerve shot to get out of trouble.

In Fig. 41, for example, the cue-ball is hidden behind the brown, with the yellow, blue and pink blocking the orthodox escape routes off a cushion.

To escape with a swerve shot, raise the butt of the cue and strike sharply downwards at the left-hand side of the cue-ball, though not too near the edge as this will result in a miscue.

Aim initially for the cue-ball to just miss the brown, so that it bends as the swerve takes effect soon after passing the brown and contacts the red as shown.

Play this with fair strength, since the most you can hope for in escaping from a snooker like this, is to put plenty of distance between cue-ball and object-ball for your opponent's next shot.

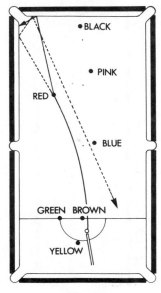

Fig. 41

Other safety shots

The colours stage of a frame often involves certain other common types of safety shot. Figure 42 is the 'full in the face' safety shot sending the yellow round off four cushions into a safe position and with any luck leaving your opponent snookered into the bargain. As the diagram shows, the yellow strikes a cushion for the third time not far from the middle pocket, so this shot is not unlike the cocked-hat double described on page 114.

There may be times when it is worth attempting this as a shot to nothing, though only if you are certain of being able to pot or play a good safety shot on the next colour.

Figure 43 is almost the same shot over the other side of the table except that you cannot hit the green full, as it would then either kiss the brown or strike the opposite side cushion and remain in the baulk area of the table. Therefore, contact the object-ball about three-quarter-ball to swing it round the angles as shown, and use left-hand (running) side to leave the cue-ball near the baulk cushion.

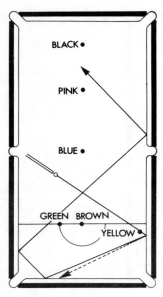

Fig. 42

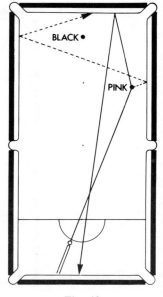

Fig. 43

Figure 44 is a favourite safety shot of mine. Many amateurs in this position play the full ball run-through, which can leave the pink near the baulk pocket. It is much safer and much more positive to play the 'crossover' shown in the diagram.

If you strike this just under half-ball with left-hand side you should, with anywhere near the right strength, get the pink near enough to the top cushion to embarrass your opponent even if you don't achieve the perfect shot shown in the diagram, with the pink dead on the top cushion behind the black and the cue-ball dead in the middle of the baulk cushion.

Be careful not to play this shot with the pink (or any object-ball) further up the table (i.e. nearer the top pocket). There is a chance, with a less than half-ball contact, of cross-doubling the pink in the corner pocket, but unfortunately an even better chance of the pink striking either the top or side cushion very near the pocket and leaving your opponent a good chance to pot it.

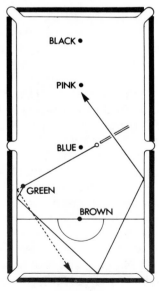

Fig. 44

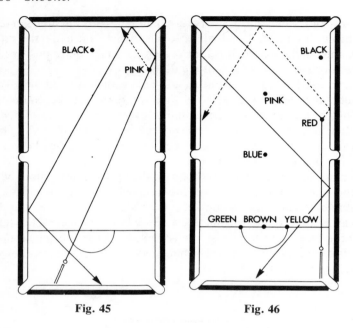

Fig. 45   **Fig. 46**

Therefore, in Fig. 45, you are more or less forced into playing the shot I advised you to avoid in Fig. 44. The important difference is, though, that in Fig. 45 the pink is further up the side cushion than it is in Fig. 44, and therefore the cue-ball has a shorter distance to travel to finish tight on the top cushion. This means that you do not have to hit the pink so hard as you would in Fig. 44 and there is therefore not so much danger of leaving it over the baulk pocket – though there is *some* danger, particularly if you are nervous.

The golden rule in these safety exchanges is to leave the object-ball near a cushion unless you are absolutely certain of leaving a snooker. If you leave your opponent the whole pocket opening to aim at there is always the danger of his bringing off a pot, but this danger is much reduced if he has to attempt the pot along a cushion, with the possibility of the object-ball staying in the jaws of the pocket if his attempt at a pot is just a fraction out.

In Fig. 46, for example, play the shot as safely as possible by bringing the blue off three cushions as shown, using left-hand side to bring the cue-ball off three cushions to the baulk cushion.

Many of these shots can be utilised when the frame depends on the black.

In clubs where the table light is operated on the meter system there is often a few minutes to spare before the light goes out and the next two players come forward to take their turn. Rather than bash the balls about with no particular object, spend those minutes usefully by tackling a game situation.

Safety in a tie-break

When a frame ends in a tie, the black is placed on its spot and the players toss a coin for choice of first shot. The first player can place the cue-ball anywhere in the 'D'.

If I win the toss, I generally take the first shot, placing the cue-ball near the green spot and aiming to go across the black, contacting it about three-quarter-ball to leave the black under the baulk cushion as shown in Fig. 47.

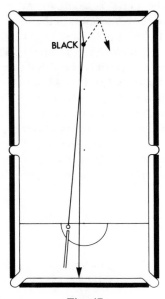

Fig. 47

The perfect shot from this position is to leave the black about a foot further along the baulk cushion towards the 'green' pocket with the cue-ball tight on the side cushion. The snag about this is that if you are slightly too hard or slightly too slow you are likely to leave your opponent a good chance of a pot.

Playing against an inferior or shaky opponent, it sometimes pays to let them have first shot.

If the black is hit too thick, a kiss will result and it is likely that an easy pot will be left; if the black is hit too thin, it will not reach the baulk cushion and the cue-ball will come far enough away from the side cushion to offer a chance of a pot in the baulk pocket.

These are the traps which you yourself have to guard against if playing the first shot. If you play it well, then you will be forcing your opponent to play against the nap (always slightly trickier than with the nap) with the object-ball under or near the cushion.

The reply to the ideal first shot is much more difficult than the first shot itself. It consists, as Fig. 48 shows, of an almost full contact on the black at just the strength to send the black past the middle pocket. If anything, it is better to err on the heavy side: not quite hard enough and the black is a gift for your opponent over the middle pocket; a little too hard makes the black a possibility but far enough from the cue-ball not to make it a certainty.

On most occasions, however, the black will not have finished tight on the baulk cushion, so it is likely that there will be a chance to play almost an identical shot to Fig. 47 in return (Fig. 49).

Another shot which is often useful (Fig. 50) is a thin safety shot, snicking the black under the side cushion and leaving the cue-ball at the opposite end of the table, ideally under a cushion.

This is preferable in this position to attempting to double the black up the table with a fullish contact; too full a contact and a kiss will occur, slightly too thin and you may leave the black near the top corner pocket.

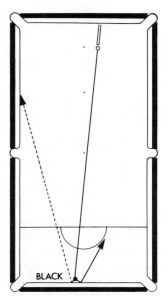

Fig. 48

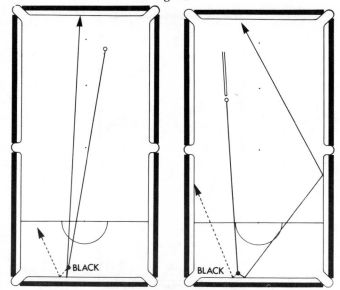

Fig. 49   **Fig. 50**

5

Miscellany and
Match Play

Doubles

Doubles are spectacular looking shots and many novices get a great thrill out of them. The most elementary double is the kind shown in Fig. 1, when the red is a couple of inches off the cushion and the cue-ball is directly across the table from it.

To pot the red in the opposite centre pocket, as shown, the cue-ball should strike the red about half-ball.

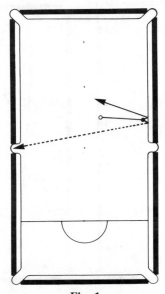

Fig. 1

This looks quite easy, and is quite easy, but professionals will still avoid doubles if they can. One reason is that it is psychologically easier to try to pot a ball into a pocket you can see rather than have to visualise where the pocket is while actually playing the object-ball onto the opposite cushion. Another is that cushion rubbers do vary from table to table, and assessing the angle for a double can be tricky. In addition, the harder one hits the object-ball, the more narrowly it tends to rebound from the cushion.

As doubles are chancy, I prefer to play them as 'shots to nothing' when possible. For example, in Fig. 2 there are two reds near the side cushion. I could play to double the higher red into the centre pocket.

The snag is that if I miss the double I am more or less certain to leave my opponent a good opportunity. Therefore, the shot to play is the lower red, attempting to double it in the middle pocket while the cue-ball travels down to near the baulk cushion, a safe position if the double fails and a good position to take the blue if it is successful and continue the break.

Both doubles shown in this diagram are known as 'cutback'

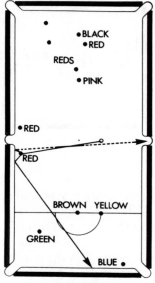

Fig. 2

doubles because the object-ball has to be cut back into the cushion to travel across the middle pocket almost along the same line as the cue-ball has taken to contact it.

Figure 3 shows a cross-double into the middle pocket which is combined with a shot to nothing. There are three reds in the top part of the table, all pottable, but the striker can only see the fourth red near the side cushion. By contacting the red just under half-ball, there is a good chance of doubling it into the middle pocket while the cue-ball bounces off the top cushion and returns into baulk.

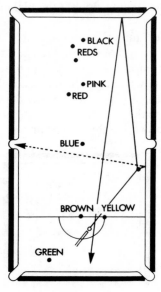

Fig. 3

If the red is potted, the green is available near a baulk pocket to continue the break. If the red is not potted, the chances are that it will bounce into a relatively safe position in the top part of the table with the cue-ball finishing somewhere near the baulk cushion.

The worst that can happen is for the red to catch the angle of the middle pocket and be thrown back towards baulk, but this is a fair risk to take.

Figure 4 shows a top pocket cross-double, a shot which often carries a greater element of risk as the near miss is likely to wobble in the jaws or at least stay near enough to the pocket to give your opponent a really good chance.

In this particular position in Fig. 4, however, there is reasonable insurance cover in the way the reds are distributed between the pink spot and the side-cushion.

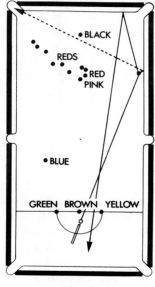

Fig. 4

If the red is potted, the break could be continued by potting one of the baulk colours or the blue into the middle pocket or, if a pot looks a bit risky, you can put your opponent in terrible trouble by rolling up dead behind one of the baulk colours to leave him snookered. If the red does not drop but stays in the jaw of the pocket, the cue-ball will still have returned down the table to deny your opponent a direct shot at that red and leave him with no other choice but a safety shot.

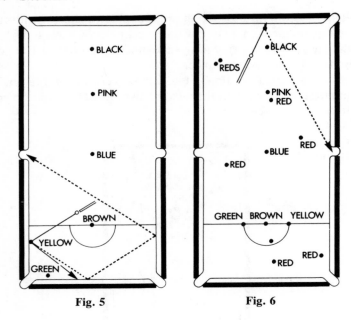

Fig. 5   Fig. 6

Similarly, the cocked-hat double (Fig. 5) is best employed as a shot to nothing. If the yellow travels off three cushions and enters the middle pocket, it should be easy enough to clear the table of the remaining colours. If the yellow does not go in the pocket it should finish somewhere near the pink which, if the cue-ball follows through to finish on the baulk cushion, as planned, should be safe enough for your opponent.

Figure 6 shows a shot I play very rarely, a top cushion double into the middle pocket. In this particular position, no red is pottable and any attempt to play a safety shot towards baulk looks doomed, as there are three obviously pottable balls in this part of the table. There is no way of putting your opponent in trouble, so it is worth trying to double the red from the top cushion into the middle pocket, a very narrow-angled shot which rarely comes off.

However, if it fails, the red should travel past the middle pocket and your opponent will only be able to play a safety shot. If the red drops, the black is, of course, in position and you should compile a good break.

This is a special case in that the reds are peculiarly situated.

Figure 7, on the face of it, looks like a similar shot even though there is only the black remaining. Here, however, I almost always prefer the very thin safety shot, as you have a very good chance to put your opponent in so much trouble, as shown, that he will have the greatest difficulty in not presenting you with an easy black for the frame.

If you attempt the double in the middle, it may well go safe if you miss it, but your opponent may not have a particularly difficult safety shot, thus enabling him to keep in the game.

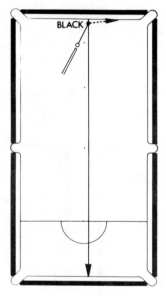

Fig. 7

Plants and sets

Another unorthodox way of potting is by a plant or set. Strictly speaking, a *set* is a position in which two object-balls are touching in such a way that it is possible to pot the second ball by striking the first. A *plant* is a position in which the first object-ball has to be driven onto the second object-ball in a particular way to pot the first.

Figure 8 shows a straightforward set. Simply use a stun shot to bring the cue-ball back a couple of inches, leaving perfect position on the black and an easy task to get position on the last red in potting the black.

You will never have an easier set than this, but even so one or two interesting incidental points arise, notably that a screw back is very easy in this position because the second red prevents the first red from going through and thus provides additional resistance to the cue-ball.

(A similar effect occurs when you find yourself playing with a cue-ball which is slightly lighter than the other balls. It has been known for sets of snooker balls to get mixed up, so if you suddenly find yourself over-screwing this is a likely explanation.)

Figure 9 shows a fairly easy plant of a type which can often be played as a shot to nothing. The two reds nearest the black are a

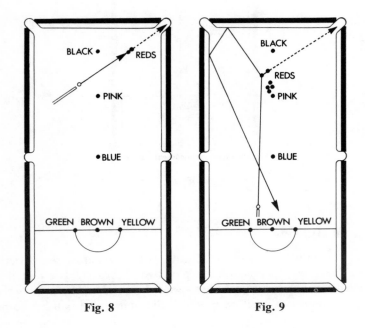

Fig. 8   Fig. 9

little apart but form a straight line with the corner pocket. There-fore, play to pot the first red as if the second is not there.

This shot is harder than a set because there is distance between the balls. With a plant, even a relatively simple one like this, the first object-ball must be contacted with a fair degree of accuracy or the second object-ball will miss the pocket.

Both plants and sets can be infinitely more complex than this. Figure 10, for instance, shows a set which does not appear to be 'on'. But, if struck in a particular way, the second red need not strike a few inches up the side cushion from the corner pocket, as would happen with a plain-ball shot.

The second red can in fact be potted by contacting the *left*-hand edge of the first red with the cue-ball. Contrary to what many people think, I don't believe that side has any effect in a situation like this.

I am not sure precisely how this happens, as the layman would probably guess that the right-hand edge of the first red should be hit; but if, like me, you are interested only in whether a car goes and not in what is under the bonnet, you will just accept that it is so.

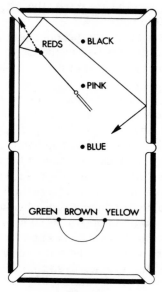

Fig. 10

Plants and sets are at their easiest when the two object-balls form almost a straight line with the pocket, but other chances often occur which are also fair risks.

In Fig. 11, the first red has to contact the second red about three-quarter-ball. You can select this angle precisely by addressing the first red as the cue-ball and then taking your bridge back to address the cue-ball.

Some players find it helpful to continue the line of their aim beyond the second object-ball as far as the side cushion. They then attempt to 'pot' the first object-ball onto the spot on the side cushion they have selected.

In the particular position of Fig. 11, a successful shot can virtually win you the frame, as the first red after cannoning into the object red will open out the cluster of three reds nearby. As you cannot get position on the black, screw back gently so that you can take the pink into the middle pocket. Unless you are very unlucky the remaining reds should by then all be in pottable positions.

Figure 12 shows two examples of the 'in-off' type of set. In the first shot, two reds are together but are not, at first glance, pottable. But if the cue-ball strikes the first red on the left, it should glance off the second red into the pocket.

The second shot shows another example of this, with a red lying against the blue and the cue-ball in the clear. Here, the red will glance off the blue into the pocket if the cue-ball strikes it on its right.

Variations of this shot providing a shot to nothing in a safety exchange are often 'on' if you look for them, although there are also occasions when you may want to take steps to avoid them, perhaps when the second red in the set is lined up not to enter the pocket but to go near enough to the pocket to leave it for your opponent.

One plant I particularly remember was a cheeky one I played in an amateur match. As Fig. 13 shows, there was no way I could leave my opponent in trouble and there was no obvious pot, so I aimed to 'pot' a red half-ball onto the brown, as shown, for it to glance off into the baulk pocket. If I missed it, I knew I would not leave him very much but, as it happened, the red went in as sweet as a nut, leaving me perfectly on the black to start an 80-odd break.

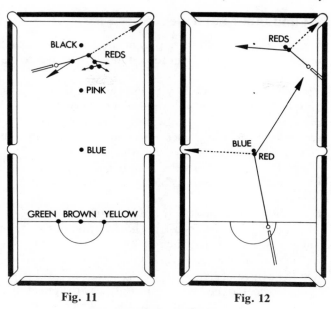

Fig. 11   Fig. 12

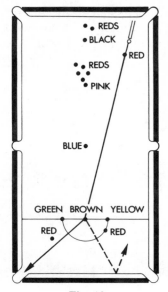

Fig. 13

The rest and other implements

I use the rest very badly and try to play my positional shots so that I don't have to use it. When I am forced into it I try not to be too ambitious.

Tall players like me don't have to use the rest as often as short players do, so I have at least got some chance of getting away with this approach even though it is obviously the wrong one.

To give yourself the best chance you need the right equipment. If a club has several rests, choose one which has a sharp X at the intersection rather than a wide U. Your cue needs to run on a straight line and this is impossible if it is wobbling about in a U-shaped rest-head.

Most club players use the rest 'the tall way up' for every shot (see Fig. 14) but most good players use it 'short way up' for some, most or even all shots. I myself use the rest 'tall way up' when I want to strike the cue-ball above centre and 'short way up' for striking the cue-ball in the centre or below.

This seems logical to me because the only way to apply top using the rest 'short way up' is to hit upwards – which seems almost impossible. On the other hand, using the rest 'tall way up' for striking the cue-ball in the middle or below will exaggerate any side you impart, intentionally or unintentionally, because of the downward action of the cue.

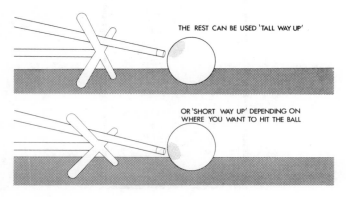

Fig. 14

When using the rest, one never has one's elbow and shoulder directly below the cue, otherwise the shot could be played with the normal bridge. The best action for using the rest is a straight push from the hand alone.

Get your eyes below the line of the shot and use only the lower arm from elbow to wrist to put power in the shot. Just as you stand sideways to the table with your normal stance, with your left shoulder pointing roughly in the direction of the shot, stand sideways to the table when using the rest, only this time with your right shoulder foremost. Grip the butt firmly with your left hand and be sure that your body is *not* behind the cue.

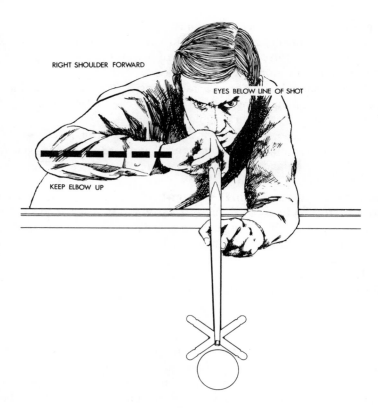

Fig. 15

One of my technically minded friends tells me that just as a tennis backhand is more difficult if the ball is taken directly in front of the body, so it becomes much easier if it is taken at the side with the freedom of being able to take a proper swing.

Another point: keep that right elbow up! Most players will find they will do a lot better if the wrist is parallel with or slightly below the elbow rather than vice versa (see Fig. 15).

As with shots played without the rest, the test of straight cueing is a straight pot. Therefore, set up a straight pot and play to stun the object-ball into the pocket. When you can do this, set up pots at a similar distance at various angles.

Spider, half-butt, three-quarter-butt

There is not much I can tell you about using these implements, since they are only for use in extreme situations. Avoid them if you can, but, if you can't, don't be too ambitious.

When using the spider – a raised rest – you will be striking downwards at a sharp angle, often when the cue-ball is in a cluster of balls with only its top part visible.

This is a situation in which you cannot follow-through because the tip of your cue would foul another red. Therefore, play with a short, stabbing motion and just concentrate on potting the red. That's as much as you can hope for.

For the half-butt or three-quarter-butt – 8ft and 12ft long rests with correspondingly long cues – the same principles as those for using the rest apply, although there is an extra degree of difficulty in using a cue much longer, much heavier or with a much bigger tip than one's own.

Try to build up a rhythm in making your preliminary addresses at the ball and don't use extremes of screw or side.

Tips

As far as tips on tips go, I haven't much to say as this is very much an individual preference. A few players actually like a spongey tip; a few like tips that are bone hard; most like something halfway between. Any tip should always be rounded to fit the shape of the cue-ball, as the inevitable result of playing with a flat tip will be a series of miscues. Some players feel more secure against miscues by using a tip which has plenty of depth in it; others, like me, prefer a tip which is almost worn down to the wafer. In fact, many of the tips I use are those which have been taken off by other professionals, who have adjudged them to be worn out.

However good or however bad you are, don't forget to chalk your cue frequently, to prevent the tip slipping on contact with the cue-ball. I chalk my cue before almost every screw shot or shot with side, and I rarely play more than two or three shots of any kind without giving my tip some chalk.

Many experienced players chalk their cue as an aid to concentration. It is no use rushing into a difficult shot. Steady yourself; get it clear in your mind exactly what you are trying to do; chalk your cue; and, having built up your concentration in this way, keep still on the shot.

Match play

If you have settled down to play a shot in a certain way and have second thoughts, stand up. Don't ever do your thinking when you are actually down on the shot. Your thinking should all be done before you settle into your stance.

The same applies to selection of potting angles. Too much alteration of the potting angle once you are down is usually disastrous. When I am properly keyed up, I always stand up and start all over again if there is any doubt in my mind. When I realise that I have missed a shot through not doing this, I regard this as one of the danger signs that my concentration has lapsed a lot more than it should.

Don't rush your shots, but don't dwell too long on them either, as you will only use up more concentration than you need to and you will never work up the rhythm which makes the game seem so much easier.

As an aid to my own concentration, I sometimes refrain from sitting down when my opponent is playing. I sense that if I start to make myself too comfortable, I may begin to feel like a spectator and start to admire what my opponent is doing, rather than gearing myself up for when it is my turn at the table.

One tip I have heard is never to let one's eyes leave the white ball, when one's opponent is at the table. I don't go as far as this myself, unless I can feel myself losing concentration, but I don't talk much to spectators between shots.

When I am actually at the table, my friends tell me, I am perpetually sniffing, coughing or blowing my nose. As I am basically healthy, these coughs and sniffs are all of the nervous variety. Once I was in the audience at a televised amateur tournament. The commentator mentioned I was there and the camera panned across towards me. Unfortunately this coincided with a bout of noseblowing so that only my eyes and forehead were visible above the handkerchief, but many of my friends assured me afterwards that they were so used to this particular view that they had no difficulty in recognising me.

This takes me to a very important point. Be natural at all times. Don't refuse a pot in a match that you would get nine times out of ten in a friendly, but, on the other hand, don't try to play above your ability just because it is a match.

Recognise your limitations realistically, play to the best of your ability and hope that this is good enough to win. If you are playing someone you feel is better than you are, relax and tell yourself that you have everything to gain and nothing to lose.

Whoever you are playing, consider the possibility that you might lose and satisfy yourself that, however unwelcome it might be, you could accept defeat. Building yourself up as favourite in your own mind only puts pressure on yourself, not your opponent.

The most nervous players are generally those who are most frightened of losing, and those who are most frightened of losing are those who, in their own minds, have most to lose.

A degree of nervousness is often helpful, as this focuses your concentration on the match. I never feel like eating much on the day of a match and would not advise anyone to eat a great deal, as heavy meals tend to make you feel drowsy and not mentally switched on.

I don't like having a last-minute rush to get to a match, but equally I don't like hanging about in a club more than five minutes or so before I play. I feel I am keyed up to play at a certain time, so I like to prepare myself for that time and stick to it.

Some players like to practise for half an hour or so on the day of the match; others don't. I don't; but if you feel it helps, do.

Contrary to popular belief, I advise you always to practise on an easy table rather than a 'tight' table. The popular theory is that after practising on a table with 'tight' pockets, all other pockets will seem easier, but it doesn't work out like that. On 'tight' tables, players have to concentrate so much on getting the pot that they haven't much concentration left for positional play. Players who habitually play on this type of table can play for ten years without extending their range of shots at all, so they never improve. Put them on a good table with reasonable pockets and they will still be unable to play more than the 'one shot at a time' game they play on their own 'tight' tables.

Whether you are winning or losing, keep to your own methods of play. Don't get too excited if you look like having a good win, because this will cause you to lose your concentration and possibly the match. If things are going badly, don't get desperate. If you're losing 0–2 in a best of five, just concentrate on the next frame and play each shot on its merits, just as if you were 1–1 or 2–0 up.

Cliché as it may be, try to be modest in victory and graceful in defeat. People *do* remember how you behave and it will do you no good at all to upset people by unsporting behaviour. These people may come to another of your matches and it must be better to have them on your side rather than against you. It's easier to play well in a pleasant atmosphere, but the atmosphere will not be pleasant if most of the people in the room don't like you.

6

The Anatomy of a Century Break

It is every amateur's ambition to make a century break. Some 40 breaks are harder to make than some centuries but, human nature being what it is, there is a certain magic in the figure 100.

There are many elements in a century break. In technique, there is potting and positional play; in temperament, there is nerve and coolness; and in factors outside your control which you could loosely call 'luck', there is the position of the balls at the start of the break, and, to some extent, the position into which they go in the course of the break.

There is no such thing as a typical century break, but there are factors which are common to many centuries, like the need at some stage to split a cluster of reds, or the problem of getting position on awkward reds near the side cushions. These factors, of course, often occur in much smaller breaks.

So, without claiming there is any magic formula for 'How to make a century', I thought that one or two useful points might emerge if I set up the balls in not too easy a position and discussed each shot as the break progressed.

I assumed that my opponent had gone in-off, so I could place the cue-ball anywhere in the 'D'. Three reds, two between the pink spot and right side cushion and one between pink spot and left side cushion, are pottable, none of them particularly easy.

However, even in a match, I would not even consider the safety shot, since there is at least a 50–50 chance of potting a red, and if I was playing well, perhaps a 90–10 chance.

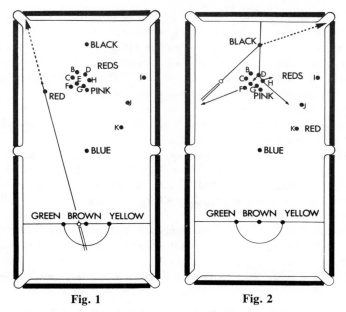

Fig. 1   **Fig. 2**

I chose the open red between the pink and left-hand cushion because a dead straight stun shot was going to leave good position on the black (Fig. 1).

Given equal distance, a dead straight pot is slightly easier than a pot on which one has to assess an angle and perhaps use a cushion. A dead straight stun pot on either of the other two open reds did not offer much in the way of positions.

I therefore concentrated 100 per cent on the pot and, in fact, played it even better than I had hoped, as the cue-ball, instead of stopping dead, ran through a couple of inches to leave it slightly nearer the black and at almost half-ball angle.

Immediately, I had the choice of playing for the two reds which were already loose (J and K) or splitting the pack with some uncertainty about the precise outcome. As the reds were not tightly packed, I decided to take the cue-ball into them using a touch of right-hand side to make sure that the cue-ball struck the right of the cluster (Fig. 2).

By striking the left of the cluster it was quite likely that nothing pottable would have been left, but I realised (subconsciously at the time) that if the cue-ball struck either red B or D or went between them, the cue-ball was virtually bound to disturb the cluster favourably. Should the cue-ball miss red D there was the possibility of potting either of the two reds already loose.

As it happened, the pack split perfectly, leaving me an easy three-quarter ball corner pocket red with the rest to screw softly across for the black.

Making sure I screwed sharply enough to avoid leaving myself dead straight on the black, I potted red B (Fig. 3, break now 9) and played the three-quarter-ball black with top and left-hand side to travel off the top and side cushions (Fig. 4) to try to hit red E full, to leave myself on red C.

In fact, I kissed red E very thinly and left myself on red D.

It could be argued that this was a slightly lucky kiss, but I would dispute this on the grounds (*a*) that a full-ball kiss on red E would have left me on red C, (*b*) that if the cue-ball had missed red E

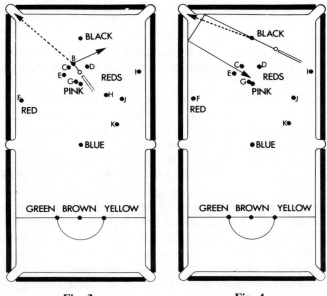

Fig. 3   Fig. 4

altogether I would have been able to pot red E into the top left-hand pocket and (*c*) that red K was pottable into the right-hand middle pocket.

I could have played red D to get on the black, but elected to screw back for the pink into the same pocket for position on red E which is obstructing red C (Fig. 5).

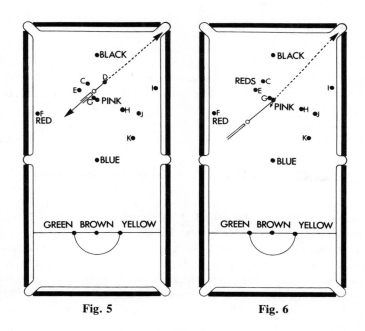

Fig. 5   **Fig. 6**

Having done this (Fig. 6, break now 23) I played red E with the rest, intending to leave a half-ball black. However, with my customary expertise with the rest, I failed to follow-through enough (Fig. 7, break 24) and therefore left myself a slightly thinner than half-ball black.

My choice was to play this pot slowly with left-hand side for red C and G, or slightly harder with right-hand side for either red J or H. I decided to try for H, since it and J were in a slightly more difficult position and it seemed a good opportunity to solve this problem now rather than later in the break. Knowing that there was a good chance of taking red J into the right-hand middle even if I was

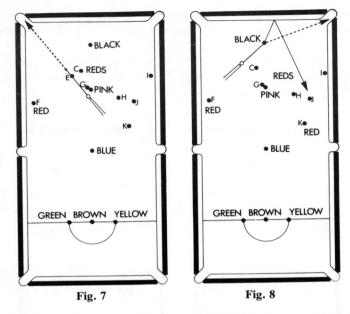

Fig. 7   Fig. 8

unable to take red H into the left-hand middle, I potted the black (break now 31) and finished on red H (Fig. 8).

Had the cue-ball stopped an inch or so sooner I would have had a natural angle to follow-through for the blue. However, since the pot was now about three-quarter-ball with no possibility of going through for the blue, I decided to screw back with a little left-hand side to take the cue-ball off the side cushion and onto the black (Fig. 9).

Again, I tried to make sure (touch and judgment are your only aids with a shot like this) that I would not finish straight on the black.

With the break now at 32, I had a half-ball black, just the right angle for the cue-ball to bounce off the cushion and kiss red F near the left-hand side cushion over the middle pocket.

At the same time, I had the certainty (even if I did not kiss this red absolutely right) of being able to pot reds C and G handily placed for the pink. It was just as well that red K was also available, since the cue-ball cannoned onto the red rather more thinly than I expected (Fig. 10, break 39).

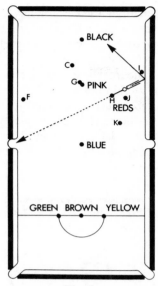

Fig. 9

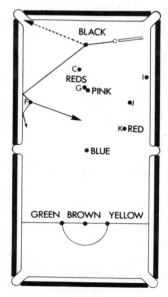

Fig. 10

This meant that the red was nudged along the cushion nearer the middle pocket but still not really into a pottable position. More seriously, the thinness of the contact on the red meant that the cue-ball did not lose much speed after contacting it.

This was how the cue-ball got much nearer the middle of the table than I expected, leaving me quite nasty thin pots on reds C and G.

For this reason I decided to take red K just under a half-ball pot with left-hand side for position on the black (Fig. 11, break 40).

This left me a perfect angle to pot the black for a plain-ball shot (break 47) and bounce off the top cushion for the two reds near the pink (Fig. 12).

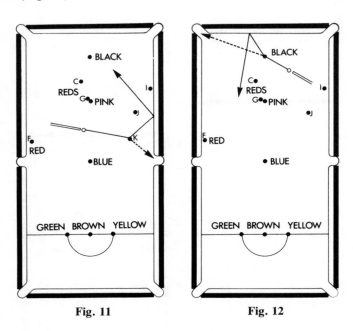

Fig. 11   Fig. 12

A three-quarter-ball stun of the red C (Fig. 13, break 48) presents no problems – although again a careless shot could leave me straight on the black.

Another three-quarter-ball stun on the black took the cue-ball off the top cushion and back on the remaining red near the pink spot (Fig. 14, break 55).

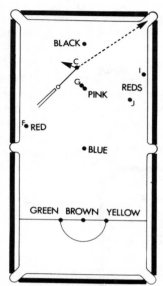

Fig. 13

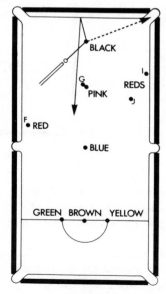

Fig. 14

I would have liked to have left another three-quarter-ball stun on this red, but the cue-ball travelled much further than I had intended and instead left me a half-ball pot.

The plain half-ball pot would have taken the cue-ball uncomfortably close to the side cushion, so I decided to strike the cue-ball slightly below centre with a touch of left-hand side (I suppose on the borderline between stun and screw) to bring the cue-ball off the top and side cushion to leave, if I could, a half-ball pot on the black (Fig. 15, break 56).

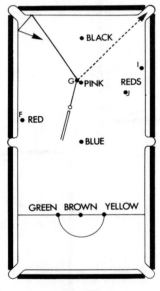

Fig. 15

I wanted this half-ball angle so that I would make a natural cannon on the red nearest the right side cushion, but honesty compels me to admit that I needed two attempts to play the shot properly.

With my first attempt, I did not pot the black cleanly, as it only entered the pocket off the side cushion jaw. This meant that the cue-ball ran through the black slightly and travelled straighter than I intended.

Whereas I intended to skim across the red near the cushion (red I), I caught it full so that a double kiss took place, the red coming back off the cushion to flick the cue-ball almost on top of red J, thus making it virtually impossible for me to continue the break.

This shows how easy it is to go wrong if you let your concentration slip, but playing the shot a second time it turned out perfectly (Fig. 16), flicking across red I to nudge it off the side cushion into a more easily pottable position and leaving me a straight pot on red J into the opposite corner pocket (break now, giving me the benefit of the second attempt, 63).

I wanted now to stun the next red J in (Fig. 17, break 64) to leave myself an angle to stun across from the pink for the red F near the middle pocket but only just off the side cushion.

I wanted, if I could, to cannon about three-quarter-ball, quite softly, on this red (red F) so that (*a*) I would not knock it past the middle pocket and (*b*) I would still have a possible 'saving' pot on red 1 into the corner pocket if the cannon did not work out.

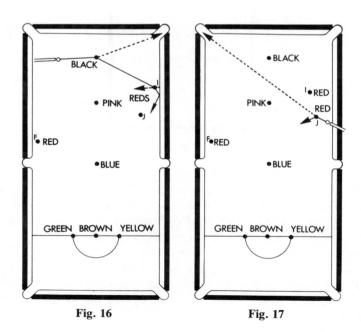

Fig. 16   **Fig. 17**

There was no need for the 'saver' as I caught red F perfectly (Fig. 18, break 70), although I quickly undid this good work by making a mess of my next shot, the simplest of middle pocket reds from which I attempted to bounce off the baulk cushion and stay baulk side of the blue to leave myself on the blue between half- and three-quarter-ball, the best angle, I thought, from which to manoeuvre the cue-ball into position for red I (break 71).

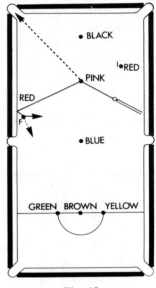

Fig. 18

As it was, I played too strongly and left the cue-ball the wrong side of the blue (Fig. 19), leaving me no alternative but to pot the blue at speed (break 76) with right-hand side to bring it off three cushions into the general vicinity of the last red (Fig. 20).

A number of things could have happened from this shot but, in fact, the cue-ball finished tight against the side cushion.

Again being careful not to play too hard and leave myself a straight black, I potted red I into the middle (break 77) and left myself about half-ball on the black (Fig. 21).

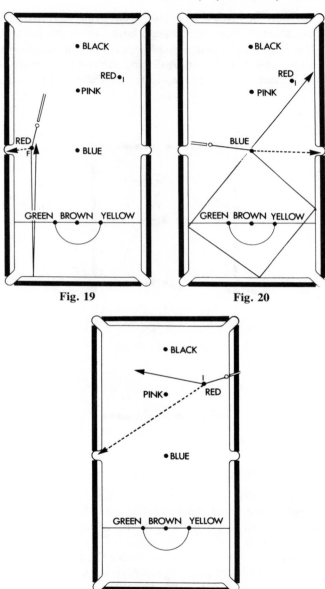

Fig. 19

Fig. 20

Fig. 21

The angle on the black is a nice one from which to stun off the top and side-cushions with a little left-hand side for the yellow, as shown (Fig. 22, break 84). The danger in playing the stun using only the top cushion and no side is that you will send the cue-ball a fraction too deep and leave it somewhere near the side cushion for potting the yellow.

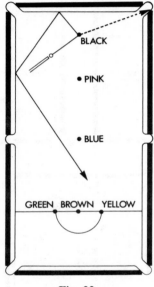

Fig. 22

I did not play this shot quite as well as I would have liked. I applied slightly too much left-hand side, so instead of bringing the cue-ball about level with the green it finished almost level with the brown, thus forcing me to use the rest.

Most good players would probably have then potted the yellow with stun and right-hand (running) side to swing the cue-ball round off the baulk and side-cushions to leave the green in the opposite baulk pocket.

However, my own preference was to play the yellow with check (left-hand) side to bring if only off the baulk cushion for the green (Fig. 23, break 86).

The cue-ball stopped almost straight on the green leaving the possibility of potting it with top and right-hand side to swing off baulk and side cushions for the brown. This is probably the most certain way of playing the shot, but my own pet shot in this position is to screw sharply across the face of the brown (Fig. 24, break 89).

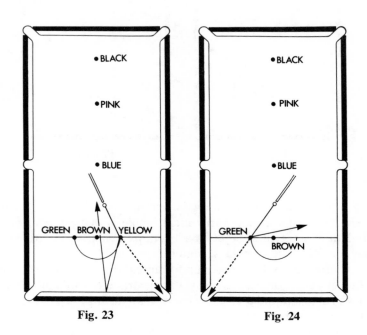

Fig. 23   Fig. 24

Barring an attack of nerves, the rest of the break from this position is plain sailing, whether you are struggling to make your century or not.

A three-quarter-ball stun of the brown off the side cushion makes it 93 (Fig. 25), a nice steady roll of the blue makes it 98 (Fig. 26), a stun pink 104 and the black 111 (Fig. 27).

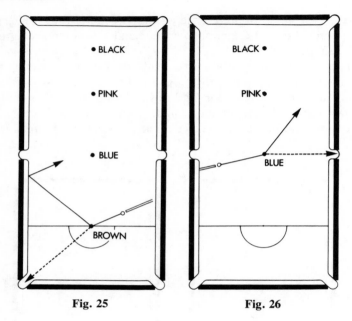

Fig. 25   **Fig. 26**

So what general points emerge from this break?

The first criticism the purist might make is that my control of strength was not all it might have been, particularly in potting the easy red E with rest or the second last red, red F.

It is often possible to make up for an indifferent positional shot with a good pot or a spectacular forcing strike, but sooner or later you will miss one and then curse yourself for having been so careless with your positional play.

To put this another way, players who are not particularly good potters have to try to compensate for this by better positional play and by out-thinking their opponents.

Looking back, I would say that the most important shot in the break was the second, splitting the cluster of reds from the first black. The cluster opened perfectly and made a great deal of the break much easier than it might have been had the pack split less kindly.

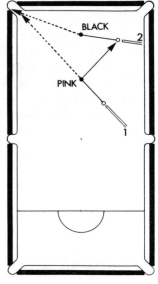

Fig. 27

Later in the break, I made a point of choosing certain reds to clear the path to the pocket for others (see Figs 3 and 7), and also tried to cannon awkward reds into better positions while at the same time retaining position on other reds (see Figs 10, 16 and 18).

Perhaps at times my positional control was not as precise as it could have been, but, except for the muffed cannon (Fig. 16), this lack of precision was not serious enough to bring the break to a close since there was always a 'reserve' or 'rescue' shot to get me out of trouble. Perhaps this illustrates the value of leaving, where possible, a range of possibilities rather than attempting to manoeuvre the cue-ball to a particular point or a very narrow area.

The latter is often possible and sometimes there is no alternative if the break is to continue, but sooner or later, one is sure to go wrong if too many shots are played with little or no margin of error.

Unnecessary striving for precision is all against building up the fluency which is so important to break-building. So too much calculation can be as disastrous as too little.

The better and more experienced a player becomes, the more he can play by instinct, since he can sense which shots call for a particular degree of control and which do not.

Play a lot. Try to learn from your mistakes. Don't be upset when your opponent seems to be having all the luck, because if you allow yourself to be irritated you will only play worse. When you're having all the luck, take advantage of it because it won't last forever. Above all, enjoy the game, because as soon as practising or playing matches becomes boring or burdensome you can abandon all hope of getting any better.

Index

Index

CHESS

WILLIAM R. HARTSTON

This exceptionally well-structured introduction guides the beginner gently from the basic moves and rules of play to a deeper appreciation of the tactics and strategy of chess.

This book contains all you need know to learn and develop an understanding of good chess. The early chapters describe the moves of the pieces, elementary tactics in attacking and defensive play, and the combinations which can force checkmate. The book then goes on to explain how to achieve control of the board in the opening stages, how to assess and exploit positional strength and weakness, and how to develop a strategic plan that will lead from decisive middle-game to conclusive endgame play. After analysing the most common opening variations, Bill Hartston then provides detailed commentaries on a series of historic games selected to illustrate different styles and strategies of play, and for their intrinsic beauty and excitement, as well as the lessons they contain.

Whether you are a complete beginner or seeking to improve your present level of play, this book will deepen your understanding and appreciation of chess, and bring new perception and pleasure to your own game.

TEACH YOURSELF BOOKS

GOLF

REVISED BY MARK WILSON

Including the complete, revised Rules of Golf

Are you a complete beginner, a leisurely weekend golfer or do you participate in competition matches? Whatever your skills, handicap or experience, this book will help you to improve and enjoy your game.

The golfer is taken step by step from choosing a set of clubs and mastering the basic strokes to playing the more complex bunker shots and awkward lies. A particularly helpful section discusses the identification and eradication of common faults. The book is illustrated throughout and includes the complete, revised Rules of Golf, as approved by the Royal and Ancient Golf Club of St. Andrews and the United States Golf Association.

An invaluable guide for those who wish to get the most out of this ever-popular sport.

TEACH YOURSELF BOOKS